MW00975105

The
Hebrew Bible
and
Science

The Hebrew Bible *and* Science

Hebrew Bible Ethics, Science, Social Life

Harry Hafner

Rutledge Books, Inc. Danbury, CT

Copyright © 2002 by Harry Hafner

ALL RIGHTS RESERVED

Rutledge Books, Inc.
107 Mill Plain Road, Danbury, CT 06811
1-800-278-8533
www.rutledgebooks.com

Manufactured in the United States of America

Cataloging in Publication Data
Hafner, Harry

The Hebrew Bible and Science: hebrew bible ethics, science, social life

ISBN: 1-58244-183-9

1. Hebrew Bible. 2. Ethics. 3. Science.

Library of Congress Control Number: 2001099115

To the memory of our mother

Batsheba Bas Itzhak Shmil

Eternal remembrance of you, Mother
who knew how to plant in the heart of your sons
honesty, justice and thirst for knowledge.
Then you kindled the torch of light and of the
Torah which you loved so much. You knew that
"Advice is the torch and law — is the light".

— Proverbs 6:23

Contents

Chapter 2 – Some Fundamental Aspects of Jewish Religion

Chapter 3 – Scientific Facts and the Hebrew Bible

Chapter 4 — Judaism and Daily Life

Chapter 5 — Judaism, State and Zionism

Foreword

On the night of November 17,1966, or Heshvan 26, 5727 according to the Hebrew calendar, our mother passed away in her sleep. Almost a year before, we discovered that she was suffering from an incurable disease: fibrillation of the heart muscle. Throughout her entire life, her heart was subjected to severe trials. Endowed with an exceptionally sensitive nature, she could never walk with indifference past what is called suffering.

As a loyal daughter of the Jewish people, faithful to piety, she skillfully piloted the family ark upon the tumultuous sea of life which was so unfavorable to our people in the world of older Europe. She spared nothing in order to give her sons an education corresponding to the demands of contemporary life, while trying to observe strictly the Jewish tradition. The inauspicious conditions toward Jewish life were not unknown to us. Yet even in those difficult circumstances, she could not sit apathetic when faced with the needs of others. Our mother was a member of the breed of Jewish daughters who knew the purposes and obligations of the woman according to our Holy Scriptures: She did not consider herself the mother of only her children and her home, but of all who are alive. To be sensitive, generous, was for her the letter of the law.

It is not surprising that every being loved her, quickly attached itself to her, and obeyed her without hesitation. When we were children we were struck by this more than once. She did not impose herself through her physical presence; rather she was small, frail, with a will and a thirst for culture; she was gentle, perceptive, and most especially, profoundly human. Any human suffering exhausted her. Any injustice disgusted her. She never forgot anyone's good deeds. Her power of judgment in complex situations was amazing. Forgiving in the face of malice, she never allowed the breaking of the Law except in cases of great need: danger to the individual or to the nation. For a person such as our mother, with her psychological framework, the heart worked to the full, faced with the continual demands which could not be avoided except through isolation. Yet we ask ourselves: would not such an isolation have constituted a danger of at least the same gravity? She should have lived longer. She deserved to be a part of more of the achievements of those to whom she gave life. However, she was able to witness the realization of one of her most precious dreams: Her sons were awarded their diplomas without compromises.

But it was too little, much too little, compared to what she deserved. Thus, while on her way to visit us, her generous, loving, much too sensitive heart could no longer synchronize its beats. Sleeping, nobody knew; nobody could have known what was happening to her. Then, as always, peaceful and silent, modest and careful not to disturb anyone, she left us forever.

What follows is dedicated to our mother's memory. We are certain that one of the things that can honor her memory is a work on a theme related to honesty and truth, synonymous with the Jewish tradition which she loved and obeyed piously, simultaneously proving that the fundamental principles of Judaism are immutable. Finally, it is a contribution toward the realization of a universal brotherhood, freely embraced, based on the profound humanism which flows from the ethics of the Hebrew Bible, much commented upon and loved by our mother.

Since deciding to write the present text, during the shiva — time after our mother's demise, many things have occurred.

Our father, Israel Ben Joseph, blessed be his memory, passed away less than a decade later, before we left our native country. The life of Marc Lawford of New Jersey, our best friend from childhood, was cut off by a cruel disease. He, together with Theodore Stein of Paris, a wonderful gentleman, helped us to smuggle the basic notes of the present little book from a communist country where such writings were strictly forbidden. Shortly after our introduction to Theodore Stein, he accepted voluntarily, without any hesitation, this dangerous mission. A terrible death cut off his life, too. We considered it would be unpious not to mention them here. Blessed be their memory, too.

— *Harry Hafner*

Introduction

The present work is a digest. Its purpose is to facilitate for modern man, caught in the rush of everyday life, a quick entrance into one of the most important compartments of the human spirit, known as the Hebrew Bible or the Book of Books. Therefore, we do not intend rendering the biblical text into a more concise form; such an action we would consider inadmissible. Rather we propose an introspection into the ethics and structure of this unique book, [1] into the lessons about and of the unique God.

If the man of antiquity could feel its profundity and dedicate himself to it; contemporary man is called to comprehend it, discovering its profound truth and beauty, useful to satisfy the human spirit and the human psychological needs. The means available to him today and the culture assimilated during more than three millennia since the appearance of the foundations of the above- mentioned book make this possible. Our text is addressed in the same degree to the faithful, to the atheist, and to the so-called "indifferent." After examining it, we hope that those in the last categories will be more understanding of the first. Taking into consideration opposition to the tenet, "Believe and do not inquire," our optimism does not seem exaggerated. No doubt the spirit of this unique work is peering over my shoulder, as I set down the opening words to examine the Hebrew Bible, a work whose content exceeds any

---

[1] The Hebrew Bible is a Book of Books as can be seen in appendix c.

human possibility to explain how it could be written such a long time ago when human knowledge about science, axiom, proof, and logic, did not exist even in its infancy.

Our little book is not a guide for travelers in a strange colorful land. It is rather an attempt to help the reader to see and perhaps sometimes to climb to endless mountain peaks or enter quiet valleys, using the roads illuminated by one of the most successful branches of science. Before we begin our travels, however, we must assure the reader that we will do whatever is possible to make his journey in the valleys or on the heights easier, and even enjoyable. We hope that at the end, their effort will be rewarded. Indeed they will find out that the Hebrew Bible is not a collection of chaotic babble, since recognizable facts, located in space and time, identifiable by scientific proof are at hand in key points of the book. During our travels we shall be guided, in each visited region, by what we call "strong science." The present work consists of five chapters containing, from a thematic viewpoint, the following elements: the investigation of facts, to make scientific analysis of known data, to use and compare ethical-moral, historical, and social facts, in order to emphasize aspects regarding concepts inside a given human social body.

Chapter One presents definitions, proofs tied to the human process of knowledge, as well as the concepts of time, axiom, and set. In our judgment, treatment of a subject which we consider to be of maximum importance should not follow the traditional, conveniently chosen models. Although models undoubtedly have their merits, in some cases the reader can be steered by them along a road which does not lead to the truth. We may, however, accept the use of models, after finding a general method of testing the chosen model and the boundaries of the area were it works.[2]

In utilizing human logic,[3] we rely on the fact that man is equipped from birth with that which we call the curiosity to know. By means of it, he succeeded in creating an apparatus which in strong science tends, asymptotically, toward precise expressions. In our opinion he is obliged to apply a similar reasoning in one of the most important domains related to the spiritual activity of the human society. As a result, what is presented here is approached in the same manner as in the exact sciences, and sometimes pure science is used to explain key biblical facts, considered by some atheists as well as some scientists as representing a flagrant contradiction between science and the Hebrew Bible. The reader will find here the existence of a close relationship among man, nature, life, and knowledge, as well as his own place in the grand universal arena. The main purpose of this chapter is to prepare the reader for the rest of the book. In order to give the user of our text the possibility to read independently each part of the book, we tried to make each chapter self-contained. Of course, such a didactic procedure requires a repetition of some facts. If the reader has a certain background, he or she may skip this chapter.

Chapter Two deals with traditional truth connected to everyday life. After the succinct presentation of some general elements relevant to human knowledge, including the books of the Hebrew Bible, the Axioms of Judaism are commented upon. A survey is made of some codes of law now known to be the oldest in the world.

Chapter Three, along with some conclusions regarding the previous sections, introduces new elements of great importance, based on scientific proof, whose purpose is to complete the content of the former chapter and at the same time to con-

---

[2] From a scientific point of view, we may call "model" a theoretical scheme that offers testable predictions.

[3] Logic is the domain of the science of the normative formal principles.

firm what the title of the present work expresses. In a way, chapters two and three constitute the core of our digest.

Chapter Four is concerned with specifics of the Judaic religion and its genesis. It takes into consideration the relationship: man, religion, and the realities of the Jewish life throughout history. A definition of the Judaic religion is given and, afterward, the appearance of Christianity and Islam is recorded.

Chapter Five presents some basic aspects regarding Judaism and the principles on which it is based. Since the backbone of the Hebrew Bible includes also legislation regarding the man-state relationship, the social-ethical aspects of such a relationship could not be neglected. In the meantime, some critical opinions are considered, together with answers based on facts. Zion and the Jewish soul, as well as other important developments that occurred in the Holy Land, the foreign domination and Arab Muslim civilizations, are recorded. The last section gives a brief presentation of the continuous link between Zion and the Diaspora as well as the return of the Jews to their ancestral homeland and to the sons and daughters of the Jewish people, who with ardent hearts and powerful arms created this path. In order to complete some elements presented in the main text and to help the busy reader obtain the needed information quickly, a postface is included at the end. Five appendixes are given with the following content:

Appendix A: The Christian version of the Decalogue

Appendix B: The enumeration of the Israelite tribes

Appendix C: A chart entitled: The Hebrew Bible, where the content of the Book of Books is given

Appendix D: Important Jewish Writings based on the Hebrew Bible mentioned in the main text

Appendix E: Some shining historical facts less known and consequently infrequently mentioned, in Jewish as well as in non-Jewish literary and historical works

Before we begin the discussion of the specified themes, the author wishes to express his conviction that the presentation of this text employs the rigor necessary for the treatment of some fundamental problems, and he hopes that the patience of the reader will be rewarded at the conclusion of the book. At the same time, he wishes to emphasize that the manuscript was tangibly improved following advice from his wife regarding the logical connection of some of the given proofs. The author wishes to give her most gracious thanks. It is also a pleasure to acknowledge my indebtedness to Dr. Melvin Sobol (previous associate professor at Pace University) who read and criticized some chapters of the Manuscript; to Ms. Adair Russell for her perceptive guidance regarding the present text, to Dr. Robert Feldman (associate professor at N. Y. I. T) for reading the manuscript and making important suggestions, to Dr. Armand Rosenberg for reading portions of the initial text, and to William Appel and Denise Sterrs for their constructive critique and guidance regarding one of the final stages of the manuscript.

One

Language is diverse; individuals are distinct but their behavior has to be directed by some rules that remain invariant in time. This means that those rules remain the same for people speaking different languages and having distinct personalities.

— Anonymous

Chapter 1

Definitions and Demonstrations

1.1

Man and Environment

From the moment of birth, the child makes contact with the surrounding world. The most intimate contact is with the mother who gave him life and looks after him. His world is a small one, but gradually it becomes larger through the establishment of new relations: family members, toys, nearby objects. The growth, and subsequently, the maturation of the individual bring on the accumulation of new knowledge, which allows it new and varied connections with the environment in which he lives.

Even though it seems surprising at first sight, man's contact with the exterior world during his existence may be expressed in the same manner, as a connection between two elements, even the amount of knowledge he accumulates with age expands continuously. Indeed, if we denote the type of knowledge regarding the exterior world as B and the type of knowledge regarding the intrinsic world of the individual as A, the totality of the knowledge he possesses can be referred to as A and B. Thus, although during a lifetime the total quantity of an individual's knowledge will increase tremendously, the number of types of knowledge remains equal to two: "I" and the exterior world.

Knowledge properly implies, however, the elimination of "I," since knowledge originating in direct experiences does not lead to universally valid conclusions, but become valid only when referred to the subject. For example, we may be impressed by a painting; we may like a perfume; we may feel warm or cold, etc., but these findings are valid for us, for our "I." Moreover, we can say that the relevant "I" is connected to the moment in which the contact between the subject and the elements of the exterior world took place.

From this point of view, the natural sciences constitute an eloquent example of that which represents an obstacle to the growth of knowledge, when everything is compared to reality. Until the beginning of the twentieth century, the natural sciences developed only by means of sensations and observations (the connections between the organs of the senses and the perception of motion, of sound, of light, of heat were direct). But the natural sciences would have become stagnant had they not succeeded in establishing a structure based on concepts which could explain, in a unified and consistent fashion, the totality of experience. Today we deal with chapters of the natural sciences that include sounds that cannot be heard, light that cannot be seen, heat that cannot be felt. What kind of world this is, we all know. It is not the world of direct contact with the sensations of sound, heat; it is the world of science which causes man to penetrate ever more deeply into nature's mysteries.

Another interesting example that serves as evidence for the importance of the elimination of the "I" in favor of the establishment of universally valid laws is Newtonian Mechanics. Isaac Newton discovered that space and time are not connected to that "I" which was previously discussed. And things remained in this condition for two centuries. It seemed that Newtonian Mechanics could be successfully used for any problem where application of this mechanics was possible. Einstein then brought new arguments, revealing the connection that still existed between the "I" and Newtonian space and time. Only after he subjected them to an appropriate analysis did the picture of the natural sciences become more harmonious. Space, which had still been connected to the subjective sensation of extent and time, to life span, became concept independent of direct observation. Certainly, the number of examples does not stop here, but their enumeration is unnecessary, since it seems evident that the gradual elimination of the "I" leads to a more precise representation of nature.

Scientific thinking developed through the centuries shows us that nature and its laws exist independently of people, and the process of knowledge cannot help people in any way to change them. These laws existed before us and will continue to exist in the time of coming generations. Ecclesiastes (one of the books of the Hebrew Bible) summarized the matter succinctly: "there is nothing new under the Sun." The destiny of mankind is to discover these laws, to understand them, and to use them for its benefit. Faithful to this destiny, Judaism, within the framework of its religious system, has consistently fought for the renunciation of concrete, anthropomorphic elements, introducing, for the first time in the history of mankind, the concept of the unique invisible and indivisible God. Addressing an enlarged human group, Judaism uses a natural language and raw data derived from observations but refined via abstract thinking, and succeeds in realizing a synthesis between abstract (unseen) and the concrete, in a universal form, valid in any social order and epoch, as we will see during the present text reading.

1.2

From Facts to Conclusions

History, as well as prehistory, have left us material proof regarding the tendency of man to eliminate the unknown from his universe. Evidently in the distant past, this universe was limited to the individual and to his immediate surroundings. In the preceding section, we mentioned how man succeeded in enlarging his knowledge, transcending the phase of direct contact. The step-by-step elimination of the unknown led him along the road to obtaining information that gradually made him master in various areas related to his immediate needs.

Concurrently with this activity, ardent and continuous, his curiosity developed. At the same time, needs arose which had been unknown to him in the initial phases of development: the need to represent, through drawing, aspects of his activity. In this way, the primitive artist succeeded in transmitting to his successors some of knowledge he acquired. They in turn, were able to perfect the methods used by their predecessors, and under new conditions, conserved and transmitted them from generation to generation. Therefore, it may be inferred that art was, from time immemorial, a means of transmitting knowledge from individual to individual, long before the advent of writing and even of language.

After numerous millennia, writing, one of the most important developments of human activity, appears. The activity of mankind then becomes more diverse. Any newly acquired elements can now be recorded with negligible effort. The possibility of compiling history, which represents the highest known form of human memory, now appears. With the diversification of human activity, the possibility of one man accumulating the total previously acquired knowledge becomes more difficult. The necessity for specialization increases, and the concentration of sustained efforts with greater chance of success in further eliminating the unknown becomes possible.

In other words, man started the full process of penetrating the unknown and felt the juicy taste of understanding the environment. This became possible only through a careful study of the partitioning of the different fields. But from a historical point of view, different fields of human activity originated from a common source of human need and curiosity, pure art being connected to the process of knowledge. The more profound understanding of some facts acquired by human experience and the possibility of conveying it in an appropriate manner begins to surround man with a certain degree of culture, and the cultured man becomes an important element of the human society. It seems that a definition regarding this new element is appropriate. *A cultured member of the human society is an individual whose knowledge acts upon his psychological framework in such a way as to orient the deepest sentiments in his possession toward a constant attachment to mankind.*

The definition seems justified, due to the fact that individuals belonging to various races, living in different places, and having peculiar customs have contributed to the flourishing of knowledge of all humanity. Culture, synonymous with the guarantee of social progress, is a product of the human species, necessarily oriented toward ascent. Culture also means power that one obtains as a backup up for maintaining one's position when faced with a brutal force. The anchoring of man to his moral force leads him finally to victory, the beast being conquered together with its entire antihuman arsenal.

History offers us such examples. Events have taken place which have extended over periods of time beyond human imagination. The owners of weak voices, having as shield and sword only the Hebrew Bible carried with them everywhere, were in the end successful. Archeological discoveries confirm this unimaginably difficult path followed by our forefathers. Corresponding to the amount of attention accorded to culture, each epoch brings its contribution to the thorough study of some fields, and therefore to the progress of the world.[4]

A certain number of new items appear. Looking at such an item more than once, for example when studying a work of art, one frequently discovers new facets. In a similar situation, we may also find ourselves face to face with a serious work belonging to another field. We usually then say that the considered items contain something hidden, cryptic. Analyzing the situation from a general point of view, we can define the amount of "crypticality" residing in a particular work. To begin with, we wish to make an observation: crypticality is a relative notion which differs from one individual to another. The amount of crypticality contained in a given work varies with each individual coming into contact with it: is directly proportional to the extent to which the creator exceeds each separate observer. This has an important consequence: *If we suppose that the excess of crypticality contained in a certain work was infinite, then the hypo-*

---

[4] By "the world" we mean the entirety of substance, alive or inert present in the universe. We call universe the whole body of things and phenomena observed or postulated. We may say, loosely, that our universe is the entire world of human experience: matter, space and energy.

thetical observer would be able to obtain limitless information regarding the work or domain under consideration. But this would mean that we would be able to attain the infinite, which is inconceivable. As a result, the mentioned amount of crypticality must be finite.

Observation

From certain viewpoints, the notions of finite and infinite are themselves relative. For example, with thought, a man can reach any distance and can take into consideration any number of items. Indeed, no matter how far he is able to reach at any given moment and no matter how many items he takes into consideration, thought can always go farther, or can take into account a greater number of items, so that the elements under discussion are unbounded. The series of the elements considered being endless, we cannot measure it and, according to the forgoing, it is infinite.

Comparing now a standard thought with a multitude of thoughts belonging to different individuals, and obliged to solve a vastness of problems in a certain period of time, it is possible to ascertain the different behavior of the individuals. Some of them will solve a number of less difficult problems; others, to the contrary, will solve another number of problems which present greater difficulties in the same time interval. Comparing the first with the second, they appear to be finite. This thought experiment shows that each thought process, within its kind, can appear as finite. Only the comparison has revealed another facet: Any body, or more generally any entity, which cannot be measured in any way, regardless of the method used to reveal its size, gives us the image of what we shall call absolute infinity. The notions of absolute and relative infinity presented differ from those commonly used in mathematics, where they are introduced through symbols which obey certain operations according to established conventions.

We have attempted to give these notions as clear a meaning as possible, since the main body of the present text may in certain points, imply such considerations in a more or less explicit form. Thus, in mathematics, the notion of minus infinity is bounded above by the number zero which is greater than any negative number, or that which we can represent with the help of negative numbers. Similarly, the notion of positive infinity is bounded below by the same number or that which we can represent with the help of positive numbers. Using the real number line we note that passage from negative to positive infinity occurs through the origin, which represents the number zero. (Fig. 1)

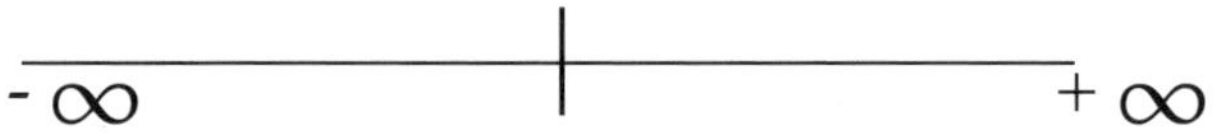

(Fig. 1)

In the figure above, the axis represents the intuitive support and the point zero the origin; that is, the point from which measurement begin. In algebra, the notion of the relative is reduced to the use of numbers affected by sign. Taking into account the character of the present textbook, we have renounced to use the algebraic explanation. However, the algebraic method is provided to the interested reader in order to show the difference between the two methods.

Even a superficial look at different astronomical phenomena makes us think about a planified construction, a blueprint of our environment, and not a chaotic one. Even the so-called natural chaos has its own laws that finally conduct to a certain order.[5] Up to about one century ago, the so-called atheists argued that the entire universe is without a beginning and without an end. As is known now, there is a proof that certainly it had a beginning. Can the creation of a human being, no matter how daring, compare to the guidance of the entire machinery of the universe, or even to the processes known today to taking place inside the living cell? During his activity of research, man copies nature and expresses some found regularities under the form of laws. But the man is a son of nature, a creation of some interaction within it, regardless of whether he is ready to admit this. He may only identify himself with his destination for a limited period of time within the process called "the circulation of matter in the universe," until the cycle ends and then is repeated.

Those who present lip research accomplish nothing. Everything reduces to a game of words around a well-chosen screen which they call science;[6] however, the mentioned lip researchers avoid the use of a scientific method in order to prove their claim. Only through the process of uninterrupted investigation via the scientific method was it possible to arrive at a high degree of abstraction and to draw general conclusions regarding the laws of the surrounding world. Analyzing the evolution of man "via the affections"[7] regarding knowledge and utilizing logic, it became possible to draw conclusions connected to the process of abstraction. This eventually leads to substantial achievements regarding how the universe works via a unique and invisible element, called in scientific language parameter, everywhere present, and named by the ancient as well as the contemporary Jews,"God" or "Almighty."

---

5 We understand by order, a condition of logical or comprehensible arrangement among separate elements of a certain group. In other words, the considered elements (out of chaos) follow certain systematic arrangements.

6 A scientific method may be based upon: 1) observation 2) reason 3) experiment. From a general point of view, we call science the application of common human intelligence to uncommon conditions.

7 Affections are considered here in the general sense of sentiments, emotions, passions.

1.3

About Eternity

The notion of eternity is closely connected to that of existence, essence, and infinity. Through the maintenance of the essence of a thing, it exists, as by destruction of its essence, it disappears. Associating the notion of infinity with that of existence, meaning the realization of the correspondence between the terms of a divergent series, for example, or the natural number line and the existence in time of a thing, we may get a glimpse of its duration, that is never finished, maintaining its eternal existence.

We have to make a distinction between relative and absolute eternity. For example, regarding the eternity of some ideas valid in a certain field, we may obtain that which we call relative eternity (since we took the considered field as a frame of reference). The validity in time of the same ideas associated with the terms of a divergent series gives us that which we will call absolute eternity. The true idea (just like the truth) is also related to a frame of reference, the field of applicability, and in this sense is relative and corresponds to its object. Only if it referred to an absolute frame of reference could we obtain the absolute truth; otherwise, the notion of absolute truth and absolutely true ideas does not make sense.

Proof

Assuming that the state of matters is contrary to what was

stated, we follow the translation into fact of a true idea. Its transposition takes place through experiment, within a given field: if the experimental conditions are preserved in that field the considered idea must be reproducible. Thus, practice would be a criterion for discovering the true idea and, in light of what was presented, would constitute an instrument for its verification within the frame of reference considered. This frame of reference, however, is a relative one, since it cannot be valid except in a particular, more or less restricted field. At the boundaries of the field considered, the validity of the true idea and of that which is obtained by transposing it into practice stops, and from this follows the relativity of the notion discussed. Each time practice indicates to the experimenter what is correct or not in the field under consideration.

1.4

The Substance

By matter, we shall mean that which can be perceived by our senses or by their extensions.[8] Please note that in order to define the substance[9] we need nonsubstance, meaning that which cannot be perceived in any way. As a result, substance and nonsubstance are united in the same way as interior and exterior, as existence and nonexistence. As soon as one of the

---

[8] By the extension of our senses, we mean various instruments or devises which may help us in perceiving some effects for which the human senses do not have the necessary possibilities.

[9] By substance, we shall mean matter proper plus existing fields. The general case is substance. We shall say about a body, a thing or, in general substance, that it is finite if it can beam measured in any way: like extent or quantity. On the contrary case, we can show it is infinite.

notions appears, the existence of the other is assumed with certainty. If one of them disappears, the other one will certainly disappear also. Thus, one of the concepts is a frame of reference for the other. When the frame of reference is missing, we cannot ascertain the existence of either of the notions considered.

From this, we may conclude that absolute notions do not exist, and all notions are relative to a certain frame of reference. Any point of the universe may be defined only with respect to another point of the universe. Because substance can exist in more than one form, by definition we shall call the various possible manners of existence of substance modes. By self causes, we shall mean various modifications or changes that intervene in substance and have the premises in the substance itself without any external interference. According to the foregoing discussion, no modification can be ascertained without the existence of a frame of reference. In passing from one frame of reference to another, we do not encounter loss of substance (except for some eventual modifications of it), which leads to the acknowledgement that substance is not destroyed, but rather continues to exist in one of its forms, meaning that it is conserved.

1.5

The Essence

We call the essence of an item, that which by its suppression leads to the suppression of the item under consideration. That which we will call essential regarding an item, an idea, etc., will refer exactly to the impossibility of its disappearance without the item, idea, etc., being modified, with respect to its most profound qualities, to the extent that it totally disappears, undergoing modifications which induce another essence.

To clarify the foregoing, we shall take an example from the exact sciences. For instance, at present we do not know the essence of the electron, but from what was said above we know with certainty that by destroying its essence we shall arrive at its destruction. Philosophical reasoning allows one to examine in a general form that of which the essential consist, regardless of the nature of the items involved in a particular case. The specificity of the particular being a part of the general, it is deduced from it.[10]

---

10 The object of philosophy consists of the generalization of results by logical clarification. This can be done in two ways: 1) verbal
2) mathmatical The first way is followed by classical philosophers; the second one is, in general , followed by analytical philosophers. In our specific problems we follow a different way. We use the results obtained by the exact sciences in order to clarity propostions regardless of the nature of the items involved in a particular case.

1.6

Attributes

We shall call attributes the specific properties of the substance connected to essence. The detection of the attributes is done by the intellect. The easier an item is to grasp as existing in a real sense, the more attributes are conferred upon it. Thus, as knowledge penetrates deeper toward understanding and discerning the essence, the number of attributes grows. Therefore, through the history of nature as a whole, the attributes do not remain invariant.

For example, the features of the animal substance have varied in time and have reached an equilibrium, explained by some on the basis of catenary structures[11] which were unstable. In the course of time, the instability did lessen, resulting in

---

[11] In the twentieth century, the mechanism of transmission of similarities between children and parents was studied. To this end, experiments were effected on plants; these were explained by assuming that each plant of the second generation receives from each of the two parent plants a determinant or a factor for each inherited characteristic. This factor was named "gene." Approximately halfway through the twentieth century, it was proven that the gene is a molecule of acid deoxyribonucleic; DNA, on short. The chemical nature of this acid and the structure of its molecule are known today. The structure of the acid can explain the mechanism through which molecules can reproduce themselves., their duplicates passing to their successors or participating in the process of growth by cellular division, each cell possessing its own structure of genes. DNA consists of units named nucleotide which are united into a linear network through chemical bonds. This linear network is called polynucleotide catenary or a molecule of nucleic acid. Now, the great importance of genes regarding inheritance of characters as well as specific illnesses, is well established.

more stable forms which we know today. In the light of the above, elaborated by using the criterion of practice applied to this field, it follows that the theory of Darwin still stands as an evolutionary theory, in the sense that the entirety of nature does not have a static character, but rather a dynamic one. This theory cannot give anything more, and the rash conclusions drawn from it may lead to inexact results.

As a whole, it becomes possible to compare it to macroscopic physics. When we aspire to a more profound knowledge, in order to approach essence, we must resort to the structures mentioned, i.e., for (today, tomorrow, possibly to something else as well) which, in turn, may give us results comparable to quantum theory in the field of physics. From that expected, hypothetical theory, causes of the profound changes intervening in our small planet and among those who populate it will possibly result. As information accumulates, it is clearer now than ever before that not the fight for existence nor the inability to adapt to the environment constitute valid arguments in the process of evolution. In light of the mentioned facts, the evolution undergone during the geological eras has been very closely connected to the attaining of a degree of maximum stability of the mentioned structures. Taking them into account, according to our present knowledge, a reasonable explanation of evolution can be given.

1.7

The Amalgamated Concept of Time-Space

From a philosophical point of view, we may say that time is a primitive form of the stream of consciousness. It gives us the possibility to separate stages called earlier and later in certain relationship to one another. A different approach opens the way to use the concept of time from a scientific point of view. Indeed, in order to link it to science, we must be able to apply mathematical relations to this concept. Then we have to have the possibility of fixing in some order of accuracy, an absolutely rigorous present, or a point of time.

In other words, the concept of time opens the way to obtain an order of relation which is a practical way of finding and making order in our world so that the stream of human experience can be classified as:

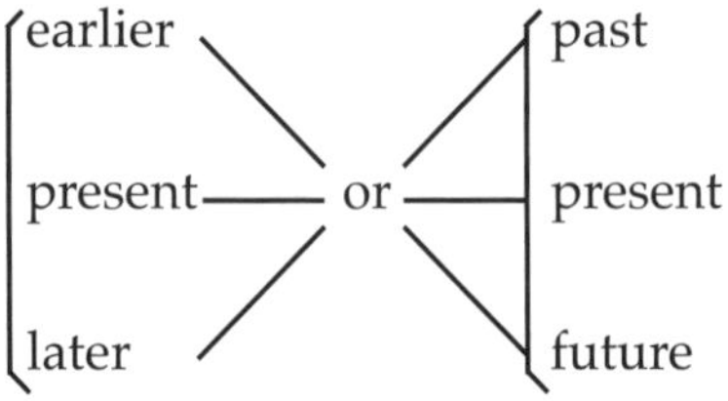

The running of the stream of time, as we specified above, can be registered, as we all know, by special devices called clocks. Such a stream, in conjunction with other natural processes, leaves a visible influence on human beings, making them alert to the detection of different events, at least at macroscopic level. On the other hand, having the ability to introduce numbers to manipulate this concept we can express the classification given above. Of course, we cannot neglect the well-known fact that we relate our lives, or the events of our lives, to the external world. And so, step by step, we reach the concept of space which is the form of external material reality.

As we can see, the two concepts time and space form a united concept where every human being develops his/her dwelling. This amalgamated concept of time-space gives us a deeper insight about events, action, and physical reality. According to daily observations, we cannot say that time is discontinuous. This can be justified by the fact that we count continuously any event that occurs with matter as well as its living, or its existence that occurs in time. In other words, time runs continuously, and any interruption does not occur. It is not possible to give absolute recipes, valid forever. To show this, it is appropriate to give an example.

For a very long time, all macroscopic bodies were considered on the human scale, the best proof for the continuity of matter. However, the knowledge acquired in time allowed us to go beyond a macroscopic understanding and showed how and when such a consideration conflicts with the physical reality. Talking about time, we cannot say that the situation is different, although up to now, the discontinuous character of time could not be established. But the running of a clock is affected by the density of matter where the clock is located. In other words, the same physical device used to measure time may indicate different readings(therefore different times) according to the place where it is located. Since the physical device used to measure time will be affected by the presence of matter, this will be of essential importance for us, when we will refer to the age of our universe.

The amalgamated concept of time-space was introduced by Albert Einstein in 1905, and the last one in 1915 by the same author. We would like to emphasize here the important fact that both were verified by special designed experiments. The last one was checked first at the solar system level. But if the Sun can stretch and distort time and space, so can a galaxy, which is made of billions of suns. As we can see, the running of a clock depends on the place in the universe where the clock is located, because each piece of matter has the property of producing what is called a gravitational field that will influence the running of a device that measures time. Then we may consider a local time as well as a cosmic time. Ironing out the differences of time by statistical averaging over the entire cosmos, we may say that cosmic time is essentially a statistical concept, like the temperature of a gas.

1.8

Affects

We call affects specific modifications of the living substance connected to the essence. Indeed, by an affective influence exerted on an individual, his behavior may undergo changes. We can be certain about any change when a comparison with his previous behavior is made (i.e. the previous behavior has been taken as a frame of reference).

Observations

1) According to the considered aspects, the affects are also relative.

2) There is a possibility of making a gradual classification of the affects, and that can explain why good things can be changed into bad things and vice versa.

1.9

About Liberty

We can say that somebody (or something) has freedom, or is absolutely free to act when its decision to perform an action started from natural necessity; and we say that it is constrained when it is determined that someone must exist and act in a certain mode.

Demonstration

The statements enunciated may be rigorously correct if, and only if, we are able to know that our decision is not determined by necessity. Usually decisions are made due to the influence of the environment that is made up of substance. We can be sure that our decision is not biased if we succeed in obviating, one way or another, whatever may influence our decision. But any decision has to be followed by an action reported to the environment, past and present and future, and that environment can be made up only of substance. Removing the substance itself, we obtain the vacuum, and the entire concept becomes senseless from our point of view (here we suppose the absolute vacuum)[12].

---

12 At the present stage of scientific evolution, the vacuum is defined as the lowest energy state of a physical system. In this way the polarization of the vacuum could be explained. By the term"absolute vacuum" we suppose an idealized situation when even such an orientation does not occur.

Then it is not difficult to find out that there is always a relative constraint to a given situation inside a certain frame of reference, and that constraint acts through the appearance of necessity. Indeed, such a situation is sometimes dictated in an affective way, being connected to some agreeable event. This is why, reported to an individual, it passes completely unnoticed. If in the same way, a state of affairs takes place that is contrary to the previous one, an individual is obliged to face new conditions. In a conventional way we call such a situation absolute constraint.

We make the following observation: Absolute freedom does not exist. The human being made up such a label for a state of affairs when his/her pleasurable situation is not modified in an unpleasant way by the dictatorship of his/her surroundings. In general, all of nature is a cradle for the human being. His life and his actions take place inside that cradle made up of substance. The multiple facets of substance with its properties furnish much pleasure and delight to the frail human creature. But when an individual is trying to impose constraints on another, and when the intensity of those constraints is sufficiently strong, it is possible to obtain a sudden modification of the substance, when even the essence can be put in danger, i.e., the human being himself.

1.10

Concerning the Creation of the World

Any material thing undergoes the following stages:

1) birth
2) maturity
3) death

Our world is a material one, and we cannot avoid the mentioned stages. Therefore, it has a beginning, a maturity and an end. All material things that make up the world were created and everyone is finite. According to previous statements, we cannot admit that the world was not created, existing by itself, the substance is infinite, without a beginning and without an end. Indeed, even our sun has a finite span of life (ten billion years). Any other star has its own lifetime according to its mass. A huge star, for example, has a shorter lifetime than a smaller one.

Demonstration

Suppose that the world has no beginning and has no end. Then such a property has to belong to all beings, since they are made up of matter too. But this constitutes an obvious negation of reality. Then, according to the last point (3), we cannot admit it (death would not exist). In such a case, only one door remains open to get out of a vicious circle: the existence of a powerful, unknown, guiding interaction that makes our universe work in an impeccable manner. Facts presented outside the general cycle of material interactions cannot be included in a rational logic. If someone tries to do this, we would dare to say: believe only in his word, but we supposed from the very beginning that we would not ask anyone to believe without inquiring. We hope that the information contained in the present chapter will help the reader to understand diverse aspects neglected at the level of understanding of a large audience and that even the restraint circle of people working in different branches of science will have the occasion to taste of the fruits of knowledge picked up from a domain which, for centuries ,some individuals have considered dogmatic. In the meantime, the reader has the opportunity to discover the close connection among man, nature, life, and knowledge, as well as his own place in the grand universal arena.

Of course, some readers may dispute the previous three points by saying that at least some things do not have an end. Also, our arguments use a certain amount of personification applying attributes of animals and people to inanimate objects and the universe itself. But cosmology, based on the known laws of physics, validates our point of view.

1.1 1

Soul and Body

The soul and body represent a unity that may be expressed through the objective real existence that may be perceived via the human sensory organs. They exist simultaneously as an inseparable unit, as long as the human being is alive. Starting with the moment of death, the soul is separated from the body. Now we give the following explanations: The soul is one of the most important consequences of the guided behavior of the human body; it elevates the human being on a higher, superior rung of the scale of achievements, imprinting in it a replica of what we call intellect. The two attributes together, soul and body, constitute the human essence. When separated, the essence is smashed and the human body reenters the general circuit of matter in the universe in an inert form.[13]

According to the Jewish religion, every individual has an obligation to his predecessors as well as to those who follow. That obligation has a source in the moral frame of the man who reached an acceptable degree of understanding of the realities of our world, and this is exteriorized by his feelings. The laugh and the cry belong to the human being and constitute a momentary exteriorization of his sentiments. We consider erroneous the interpretation given by some writers, philosophers, etc., who condemn the moral according to which even the tears are virtues. For them virtue means power, and tears mean the

---

13 We may say that, from a chemical point of view, any metabolic process stops.

exteriorization of a human feeling as an expression of weakness. There follows a legitimate question: When you cry after a loved one, a parent, for instance, are you doing it as an expression of weakness or of love? Those who have passed through such situations know very well that the age of the loved one doesn't matter. A loved one is ageless. You feel as though something in your body had been broken and, as a result, a lot of pain follows and tears will appear in your eyes. According to the aforementioned interpreters, the love that we talked about seems outside nature, but in our opinion, somebody incapable of feeling is abnormal or, more precisely, perverted.

1.12

Research, Truth and Faith

Any scientific research has the purpose of establishing in the best possible approximation some phenomenon, the conditions in which they appear, their origin. In addition, we can say that irreducible ethical rules, well established by human experience, can never be in contradiction with scientific research and its results. We suppose that this is obvious, because the research itself is supposed to be directed in a way that conducts the researcher on a right track, since practice is, finally, the only authorized judge. Of course, some individuals may have different points of view in the process of experimental data interpretation. That depends on the possibilities of every researcher: his power of judgment, his cultural background, etc. The different interpretations of the same data can be eliminated only by a strong scientific knowledge of reality in different compartments. Then and only then, the lack of agreement can be eliminated. In other words, the human knowledge is a fortiori, divided in compartments.

Demonstration

Any individual, according to his background, in a certain period of his life can reach the truth in a compartment related to a specialized branch of science. If that were not true, then it would require a branch of science specialized at the level of the entire universe; as far as we know, such a thing doesn't exist. The existence of a compartmental division then follows with necessity. From this we may conclude that a human being can obtain, during his life, a partial knowledge connected to a particular domain only, whether he likes it or not.

As we mentioned already, he who works in a certain domain is using the experience of his predecessors, and based on that experience he is able to go forward. We are in the same situation, and we will try to show how this applied to ourselves. What I took from our forerunners cannot be framed into the patrimony of the ancient or modern philosophers well known in the universities of Old Europe. Based on the process of transitivity, and sometimes maybe directly, I took over some Cartesian ways of reasoning, but mainly they belong to Spinoza because of his specific way of analyzing that was familiar for me from two points of view.

1) Being Jewish, I have the same inheritance in the Talmudic style used to solve a problem, a method that can be found at every step in Spinoza's work (even if we disagree with him sometimes).
2) According to our background, the analytical way of thinking must be familiar to us because, without it, is it impossible to move forward in the domain of knowledge. Our permanent

guide was that Judaism had never said, "believe and do not search."

Celebrated theologians, like Ibn Ezra, who worked to create a scientific base for the theory of numbers, and Reb Moshe Ben Maimon, known under the name of Maimonides, were present in the frontline of the great researchers of nature. For instance, Maimonides was considered as the spiritual leader of the entire Jewish world, and he was in the meantime one of the great physicians of his time, as well as a mathematician and astronomer. Spinoza in his masterpiece *The Ethics* tried to find among other things a scientific foundation of God's existence using the knowledge and methods of his time.[14] With that purpose, he starts with the basic observation about the surroundings; namely, a human can detect the presence or absence of something via his sensory organs. But only material things can be detected in this way, and an empty universe, without matter, was for him, as for anybody else, impossible to imagine.

He tried to analyze the entire world from this point of view, and reached the conclusion that the Creator makes its presence felt via the different manifestations of the matter existent in the universe. In all Jewish religious works based on the fundamentals of the Hebrew Bible, which is the Torah, the commentator recognizes that a unique guiding interaction has created from the very beginning material things, as well as their characteristic behavior. What we call a miracle in a certain moment, is due to the impossibility of our ability to explain certain things, in certain moments of our life; however, they were established from the moment that our material world came into being. Therefore, what we now call the laws of nature are precisely mentioned in the Hebrew Bible, using the language of that time. No myth or saint who can perform mir-

---

[14] Even his points of view were different at different stages of his findings, as is true of a researcher when performing his work.

acles that are alien to the natural world. What some commentators have added to the Hebrew biblical text, like that God imprinted in the created human being his own image, has absolutely nothing to do with the text of the Hebrew Bible. It is, rather, related to the human experience, which emphasizes the anthropomorphic origin of such a statement.

Indeed, as we know, a man can create a man after his own pattern. This represents rather the echo of the prototype of creation through which those commentators believed that God created the human being after his own image. It was a way of helping the simple man on the street understand more easily some abstract notions which, only after thousands of years, we are beginning to appreciate. To better understand why the commentator introduced such a comment, it may be sufficient to mention that Judaism strictly forbids prostration in front of any image or human element, regardless of the role played by the person even in the foundation of Judaism itself. It also strictly interdicts kneeling down, even in prayer, in front of the Almighty, saying with absolute clarity that God forbids such an act, since it constitutes a humiliation of his creature, the human element the crown of His creation.

1.13

National, Universal and Individual Creativity

Let's say an artist wants to realize a certain painting. The question is: how can he paint the environment in such a way that the resulting work will represent a piece of art? The answer to such a question is a difficult one, since the result will depend on the sensibility of the artist, the exciting factor, and finally on what is called the artist's talent. Using mathematical language, we may say that the representation of an artistic work is a function of the mentioned variables (exciting factor, sensibility, talent) and that their proportion varies from one artist to another, via the process of creation. The great masters displaced their private experience in certain conditions of freedom that influenced the entire previous lifestyle. This may depend on a specific national frame of reference and on the artist's education, which is transformed in generating seeds of new bonds, with profound and multiple resonances in the human nature. The seed, the result of a master's experience, can be compared within certain limits, to a concentrated energy that needs time to be released.

Looking at a true piece of art, let us say a painting, we discover more and more about the subject; every pigment of paint acts as an exciting source of messages transmitted to the viewer. If we are able to sum up the artistic work involved in such a painting, and judge its action on viewers in time, we may find an enormous quantity of energy concentrated in artistic form, and its powerful action on the people analyzing it. The human strings start to vibrate when such energy is released.

One obtains the accord of the world's human community which considers it a common treasure.

Usually, the aforementioned master uses in his creativity something specific to the nation to which he belongs and inscribes himself fortuitously on the creativity curve of universal values. For example a great writer, even if he treats a particular case, takes into consideration the existing possibilities and, in the meantime, touches upon problems of general importance that may include collective humanity. After a great military victory, he may write a poem to glorify the soldiers of that nation; simultaneously, he may make a synthesis of the great victories presented in their essence and belonging to different nations. The resultant piece of art will contain the generalized boiling life of the writer's epoch projected in the future toward other, different epochs.

In a certain moment, each of us is located in a well-defined place on our planet. His/her starting point, the epoch, education, country, and background form a specific configuration located in a frame of reference. If the piece of work does not undergo any changes in its essence when we pass from one frame of reference to another, then we obtain a piece of art of universal value. Otherwise, the result of the artist's work will classify the creator as being of local or national value only. However, some representative writers at national level succeeded in obtaining, at the same time, universal recognition after they made known to the entire mankind true treasures of art, belonging to their people, or to those people among whom they made their living. This shows the possibilities of some individuals of unusual talent to create values included in the continuous humanitarian circuit, using their proper frame of reference[15].

---

[15] It is well-known that the great composer Ludwig van Beethoven created a symphony called *Eroica* to glorify one of Napolean's victories. Today, that piece of art is considered a common value of the entire human society.

Therefore, passing from one frame of reference to another cannot affect, in any way, a created value, since then we may say: It remains in general unchanged, or invariant.

In conclusion, to check the validity of a piece under scrutiny, on a valoric plane, we have to pass it from one frame of reference to another. For the moment only, it is enough to consider the basic concepts of the Hebrew Bible passed from one epoch to the other; each one being taken as a frame of reference. As practice is shown us in a vivid way, it passed successfully through: slavery, the Middle Ages, capitalism, and even the passed away communism was not able to change an iota of the Book of Books.

1.14

The Concept of Axiom

In general we call axiom a maxim widely accepted on its intrinsic merit. From our viewpoint, we need to melt down human experience on a large area and to reshape it in a concentrated manner; then it becomes an assumption on which a logical argument can be based. The new form obtained, opens a way to use that reshaped experience as a base for a certain domain of science. This is the modern approach in physics, a branch of science which, up to this moment, remains as a model for all other branches of science by its ability to explain and generalize known facts and to predict physical observations previously unknown. It has nothing to do with esoteric acronyms.

1.15

The Notion of Invariant

Among other things and concepts, we used in the present chapter several times the notion of invariant. Since we will meet it again, we wish to explain it in some detail. The mentioned expression is a connection ring between considerations of psychological order and the exact sciences. Its origin belongs to analytical geometry, where it has been used to determine from a quantitative point of view, spatial configurations, that represent simple bodies or sets of such bodies. Eliminating nonessential aspects from the analytical description one obtains the so-called invariants, which describe only what is essential in the figure under consideration. The method maintains its validity for other compartments of research where/when we look for the elimination of the nonessential. What remain are the invariants that describe the object. Through an extension of the notion, one can say that the invariants constitute a connection between the naive and scientific way of thinking, ensuring that we obtain the essential in a considered problem.

1.16

Sets

We call set, a collection or group of things having the same nature. For example, all books belonging to a library form a set. Their common nature consists in the fact that all of them are books. Using the same definition, we may talk about the set of all stars or galaxies. Their size, brightness, or chemical composition doesn't matter. We are interested in the fact that all of them have the same nature: They are stars, galaxies, etc. The objects of the same nature making up a set are called members or elements of the set.

A set may have a finite or infinite number of elements. There is an entire mathematical theory of sets invented by George Cantor (born in Russia in 1845 and lived in Germany much of his life, where he died in 1919). He introduced in mathematics the first letter of the Hebrew alphabet, aleph, used ever since for the same purpose used by the author. The theory of sets, ridiculed by some researchers during Cantor's lifetime, invaded, in our days, practically all branches of mathematics. A set that is of special significance in the development of set theory is the empty set. The empty set is one that contains no elements. It is conventional to agree that the empty set (notation $\emptyset$) is a subset of every set and it is present in any set. With sets, are introduced operations with like numbers.

We are not going to develop further the theory of sets. We use the concept of sets to emphasize how and why the human being is influenced by nature, and how he acts on the surroundings to use nature to his advantage, or at least as he believes it to be to his advantage at the time.

1.17

Sets and the Natural World

The entire human society forms a finite set. But each element of that society is a part of the entire nature to which all animates and inanimates belong. According to this point of view, the entire world is built up by certain sets. The surroundings and their geographical location have an important influence on the entire life of a certain region: human beings, trees, animals. The entire climate of the region is dominated by its geographical location. The set of human elements is the only set able to counteract adverse natural conditions, to adapt and conquer new territories not too auspicious to human life. These changes are local, and cannot affect the entire natural world in a global way; rather, it continues to develop according to well-established laws.

Therefore, we may say that the world is not a chaos, but rather a cosmos harmoniously ordered by well-defined laws discovered step-by-step by man employing mathematics, invented by the same human element using his mind. But mind is freedom applied to a set of finite situations within the limitation of its existence. It is an open set toward the infinity of daily active enterprises, since each generation continues the work of the predecessors. As we can see, these sets together and their interaction represent the essence of man himself.

Of course an important question may arise: How was it possible for the frail human element to do such a tremendous job? First he discovered the laws of thinking, long before they were written down by some philosophers. This was possible because of the structure of the entire material world, which acts on him as well as on all other parts of the same world. This kind of action is done according to certain laws that imprinted in the human mind the laws of thinking, a certain order called logic (a more formal definition was given earlier, in footnote 3). So we could realize how all parts of the universe have a continuous connection and influence on each other.

As we shall see later, Jewish religious belief centers around two main issues: the first one is cosmic in character and it shows the human dependence on and connection to the universe; the other one emphasizes the moral dignity, the individual human responsibility within the autonomy of each member of the human set established by certain basic rules that remain invariable in time. So through an intellectual approach based on active contemplation, thinking, and abstraction, the perfection characterized by its ability to manipulate the steering wheel of this ordered world has been discovered and called, because of this, the Almighty, in order to underscore its possible activity.

Interesting is the fact that such a tremendous discovery was made by our ancestors approximately 4,500 years ago. The individual element of the human set made every possible effort to discover and understand more and more from what the abstract supreme perfection did. This difficult way gave birth to what we today call science, a field in which some researchers got the impression that they succeeded to crack down the barriers between the human element and that which is called divine intellect. From a historical viewpoint, the presence of the divine and how it manifests itself has been explained by humans in two different ways:

1. The omnipresence of a supreme power in anything of our world (the Hasidic point of view), mentioned by Spinoza in his masterpiece Ethics more than one hundred years before the existence of the Hasidic movement.

2. The lawfulness of nature discovered via mathematics, fascinated the great scientist Einstein by the order that exists in the natural world. His statement, "God doesn't play dice," became known worldwide.

Even from our short presentation, it is possible to see that science is not at all removed from what was defined thousands of years ago by the name of Almighty. With a relatively simple analysis made in chapter three, it will become possible to ascertain that extra-human knowledge was needed in order to obtain a true treasure of knowledge for all of mankind from that remote time. We do not blame, outcast, or characterize in one sense or another any religion; this is absolutely out of the question. Everyone is free to believe what he/she wants, and in whatever way he/she likes. The only statement we make, without any doubt or remorse, is the following: If a system (scientific, religious, philosophical, or whatever) is not based on an invariant group of statements, that system cannot endure throughout the continuous development of human history. Of course, it can be maintained by terror, for a while, but its final breakdown cannot be avoided. It is worth noticing that the action of different sets of factors which seem to belong to different fields interact in a way that finally results in something new and unique that is superior to previous stages. In other words, even what we call chaos has a certain hidden organization, as though to conduct the researcher toward what we may call antichaos.[16]

---

16 See also Stuart A. Kauffman *Scientific American*"Antichaos and Adaptation," (August 1991),p. 78.

Two

The revelation at Sinai asserted the supremacy of ethical life and the dignity of man, and is generally considered to be the cornerstone of Judaic beliefs and values; its moral base has not been exceeded after more than 3,000 years.

— Anonymous

Chapter 2

Some Fundamental Aspects of Jewish Religion

2.1

Introduction

In every member of the human race lies the tendency toward freedom, and connected to it, the desire to do whatever he likes. From time immemorial, such tendencies have appeared under different forms. In our era the advance in knowledge in the civilized world has become larger and deeper, and every new discovery makes the self more confident in its possibilities. With every new discovery, man's feeling of security increases, and usually his curiosity increases too. In the complex process of learning at "the school of life" and the large successes obtained, an interesting interaction between student and environment takes place. The timidity of the beginning starts to vanish and step-by-step we discover that the student of yesterday has became the modern researcher of our time. Every discovery has its own history, with big successes and sometimes with equally large failures. But perseverance is necessary if progress is to continue. In the following, we try to make a "tour de force" through the ethics of that age and to establish a first intimate contact with our epoch. In this way, we hope to be able to show, in a convincing way, to the contemporary man that his "detachment" from his ancient kinship is a relative one, and that the quintessential elements of decent behavior were established long ago and cannot be modified even after several millennia. As mature members of the human society, we are called upon to fathom their meaning and apply them to our lives. In the following section, we are going to present the Ten Commandments, and show how they constitute an ironclad system checked by millennia of practice. This is necessary, because the original Ten Commandments constitute the backbone of Jewish ethics and of Moses' Books, the fundamental of Jewish belief, known under the name of torah.

2.2

The Hebrew Bible and Its Books

In the process of daily fight for his existence, the human element is obliged to find new ways of acquiring what is necessary for his survival. In this strenuous effort he accumulates experience, his vision is enlarged, and he tries to explain for himself certain phenomena. Such ways are used by contemporary researchers, and they were used by our ancestors too. Some contemporary historians and critics are looking for tangential points between Judaism and the religions, customs, moral standards, and organizing systems of other populations. According to well-known facts, one civilization can effectively influence another. By direct contact, a reciprocal interchange takes place, and eventually the influences are incorporated into each culture. An unusual thing comes to the observer's eye when he has reached the terminal line of analysis regarding specific occupations, trade elements, etc., and he finds himself suddenly confronted with a completely different situation: the Jewish culture, dominated exclusively by religion.

One notices that in other cultures, the character of religion isn't as sharply dominant as it is in Jewish antiquity. Some observers have shown that as a consequence of such an orientation, the entire Hebrew literature was absorbed by editing religious texts. The basic book of the Jewish religion is the Hebrew Bible, which is comprised of thirty-nine books. The critics of the Hebrew Bible presented those books as a result of a secular work carried out by entire generations of Jewish writers. Such a statement, which seems to have a certain logic at first glance, has been refuted by archeology, which has discovered the existence of literary works which are not included in the Hebrew Bible. In the Book of Books, the guiding thread is represented by events, judicial standards, and the wisdom of the ancestors included in the unfolding history. But what is the structure of the Hebrew Bible? What books are included and in what order? The Hebrew Bible has the following main divisions:

1. At the beginning are the five books of Moses, known originally under the name of "torah." The name "torah" denotes study, learning, culture. The first of the five books is Genesis. This is a Greek word and means "the origin or coming into existence;" the Hebrew name for this book is Bereshit. Genesis covers an unthinkable period of time. It starts with prehistory (the beginning of our world) and it brings us into history. In the same book, the formation of an ethnic nucleus is considered with Abraham as a father. The Hebrew ethnic nucleus migrated on the piece of land located between the Arabian Desert, the Phoenician Sea, the river of Egypt, and the Euphrates River. From here, the patriarch Jacob with his sons left for Egypt because of some unfavorable meteorological conditions.

The second of Moses' books is Exodus. This is a Latin word which means "going out". The Hebrew name is Shemoth. An important part of this book is dedicated to the Jewish law received on Mount Sinai. At this point appears the giant figure of Moses, leader of his people, organizer, and diplomat. He succeeds in freeing his people from Egyptian bondage and leads them toward the land promised to Abraham, Isaac, and Jacob.

Taking into consideration the value of human labor in a society dominated by slavery, it is inconceivable how the

Egyptian monarchy could allow 600,000 slaves to leave without any military confrontation.[1] It is a fact enveloped in great mystery for the unbeliever, a miracle for the indifferent, and the presence of the Almighty for the believer. Such a fact cannot be explained from a purely rational point of view. Every slave represented a certain value and no one would willingly give up such a treasure — more than half a million slaves.

The long journey toward the Promised Land is described in the next two books, Leviticus and Numbers. Leviticus is also a Latin word that means "priestly." It contains the laws of the priests and the Levites. The Hebrew name of this book is Vaykra, meaning "and he called." The first sentence of the book begins with this phrase and that is how this book got its Hebrew name. Numbers is the fourth book of the Torah. Its Hebrew name is Bamidbar, meaning "in the desert." It describes the experiences of the Hebrews in the desert, on their way out from the country of bondage, Egypt, toward their country of freedom, Canaan.

The fifth book is known as Deuteronomy, and derives its name from the Greek word "deuteronomion," which means second law. It is the last book of the Torah. Its Hebrew name is Devarim, meaning "the words," taken from the opening of the sentence of the book. This book is a restatement and a revision of laws as given in Exodus, Leviticus, and Numbers, and it tells of the death of our greatest teacher, Moses. Moses, the titanic diplomat and fighter for equality, righteousness, and brotherhood among men, isn't allowed to step into the Promised Land. He left a series of dispositions that will be used by his followers. Their immediate application has been

---

1 We are in the possession of a mathematical proof based on the Malthusian Law that shows the Jewish caravan going out of Egypt was made up of 600,000 people.

done by Joshua, the military commander chosen by Moses to organize and prepare the army of the twelve Israelite tribes, which had to be used to defeat the eventual military resistance of the Hebrew enemies.

The second main division of the Hebrew Bible is called the Prophets; in Hebrew, Neviim. This division is divided into two parts:

1. The earlier Prophets contains the following six books: Joshua, Judges, Samuel I, Samuel II, Kings I, and Kings II. Here we find the history of the Hebrew people from Joshua through the Judges, of Saul, David, Solomon, and of the division of the kingdom, the fall of the northern kingdom in 722 B.C., and the fall of the kingdom of Judah in 586 B.C.
2. The later Prophets section contains fifteen books and consists mainly of the sermons the prophets preached. These books are: Amos, Isaiah, Jeremiah, Ezekiel, Hosea, Joel, Obadiah, Jonah, Micah, Nahum, Habakkuk, Zephaniah, Haggai, Zechariah, Malachi.

The third main division of the Hebrew Bible is called the Writings, or in Hebrew, Ketubim. Here we find: Psalms, Ezra and Nehemiah, Proverbs, Job, Song of Songs, Lamentations, Ecclesiastes, Ruth, Esther, Chronicles I, and Chronicles II. In the Writings, we find the most important moments of those Jews who came back from the Babylonian Exile to rebuild the ruined country and first of all the Temple, one of the greatest pieces of art and splendor of that time, the house of prayer for the unique invisible God. These facts are described in the books of Ezra and Nehemiah.

In the same section are included books belonging to the lyrical genre. An important group is the collection of psalms mentioned above, consisting of 150 pieces of lyrical poetry that express the highest and profound feelings for the divinity. A misunderstood lyrical work by the so-called critics of the

Hebrew Bible is the Song of Songs. Due to its form of presentation, this piece of poetry has been considered by some critics as being profane, and they still cannot understand how it could find a place anywhere in the canonical Hebrew Bible. Sometimes they scoff at the pious people, saying that only a lack of knowledge about the content makes them speak with great respect about that text. In the pages of the Song of Songs, one of mankind's greatest poems, is described the delicate feelings of love of a young shepherd for a shepherd girl, using accents of an exceptional tenderness.

Some critics judge this work completely out of context. If they read the Hebrew Bible up to this point and didn't understand its message, obviously it would be hard for them to understand the Song of Songs. From the pages of the Hebrew Bible, it is crystal clear that man has to approach holiness through pure, gentle feelings. In the same pure way used to pray to the Almighty, he has to approach human beings and nature, without any hidden desires behind his words. No lip words are admitted, only heart words, so to speak, have to be used. This is why the Song of Songs could find its place in the canonical Hebrew scripture. Even the name, Song of Songs, indicates that you have to sing gentle feelings for your fellow man, God's creation, as you do for your Creator, but don't forget what is written in the Ten Commandments: Your God is unique. The entire attention of the Hebrew Bible is focused toward the human social element, and the purpose is to elevate his spirit and to polish his feelings.

We should mention here the Jewish custom before the day of atonement, one of the most important days of the Jewish calendar. On that day, the religious Jew can obtain forgiveness for sins committed toward the Almighty only. If he sinned toward a fellow man, then he must ask that man to forgive him; God cannot grant such a favor. The honest feelings toward your fellow man reach a climax of the divine congeniality, which is in full accord with them and support them. Nothing is forgotten when it is a matter of promoting a peaceful understanding, friendship, and sympathy toward the weak. God keeps the scale of righteousness inclined toward the defenseless, and such honorable behavior is required from each man.

Finally, there is another group of books in the Hebrew Bible that belong to the didactic style, the writings of wise men (see division III of appendix C). All three divisions of the Hebrew Bible were written in Hebrew except the book of Daniel and a part of the book of Ezra. These were written in Aramaic, a semitic language similar to Hebrew, at one time used by the Jews in everyday life and in some prayers.

We cannot conclude this section without presenting a critical point of view of a German researcher and critic of the Hebrew Bible, Julius Wellhausen. From his point of view, the order of the books contained in the Hebrew Bible has to be changed. The Jewish tradition considers that the Pentateuch (which means Moses' Five Books) was written by Moses and that is why it is at the beginning of the Hebrew Bible; it corresponds chronologically to the events recorded. The second main division, Neviim has been considered also according to a historical chronology. So is the third main division considered

---

[2] Not all Hebrew writings are included in the Hebrew Bible. Starting with the day when the Temple of Jerusalem was destroyed by the Romans, via arson, the Council of Jabne of seventy–one scholars under the leadership of Dr. Johanan Ben Zakkai established the borders of the Holy Scriptures. They decided which writings would remain in the Hebrew Bible. Ben Zakkai considered that this remained from Israel's kingdom, and had to be guarded. The books were considered the provinces of the Jewish people; the chapters, paragraphs and the rows, the cities, villages, and hamlets of the Jewish people. The military facts of the Hasmoneans, great fighters for freedom of their people, implacable enemies of idolatry, were not accepted as a part of the Jewish Canonical Law. The spiritual kingdom, build up by seventy–one erudites, proved to be stronger and more enduring than the Roman Empire.

to be in the right place. The Christian tradition takes over the structure of the Hebrew Bible[2] (changing one of the Ten Commandments) and including some books excluded from the Hebrew Bible.

The presented tradition came under critical fire starting in the eighteenth century; the sharpest and most exhaustive presentation, according to some critics, has been made by the aforementioned Wellhausen. He considered Moses' books to be the result of a combination of different heterogeneous sources written a long time after Moses. In order to justify his statements, Wellhausen and his school analyzed the difference in language and style of the mentioned books. The conclusion was that the order of the divisions of the Hebrew Bible must be changed to reflect the chronology of historical developments. Thus, the books of the prophets and different historical data, according to his analysis, are older than Moses' books. Wellhausen considered these books to have been written during the Babylonian Exile. He and his school had the feeling that they discovered the impulse needed by the Jews to present the Hebrew Bible in a certain order, their separation from the homeland.

All atheistic groups were fascinated by the splendor and subtlety of Wellhausen's criticism. All those who tried to find a logical order for the books of the Hebrew Bible adhered to his point of view. None of them raised the objection: What text was used in Wellhausen's analysis when such a conclusion was reached? An answer had to be given, but this wasn't an easy task. First of all, archeological research was needed. From a theoretical point of view, the task wasn't difficult. Once the archeological research has been developed, step-by-step, that great success of Wellhausen's findings lost more and more ground. Under the increasing pressure of new archeological discoveries, the modern critic was forced to give up the essential aspects of the quoted school and to restate the Jewish tradition.

Today it is recognized that the writings of the Hebrew Bible follow the historical developments up to the second century before the modern era. The explanation for Wellhausen's discoveries are simple. First we have to recall the fact that the Hebrew Bible has been copied by different generations many times. Over time, even the meaning of some words has been changed, and the scribes or translators gave different meanings to certain expressions so that the truth could be established only by examining a text closer to the original.

On the other hand, Wellhausen and his entire school neglected a very important fact recorded in Jewish history: Before the Jewish Babylonian academies started to work, the Jews were not preoccupied by the grammar of their language. After the grammar had been made up, all Hebrew canonized texts were rewritten, introducing the required corrections. Evidently, every writer had his own style, but this is not important at all. The most important thing was to leave to posterity an unmodified content of the Hebrew biblical text. The information contained in the original was transmitted. We may say, without exaggeration, that by its content the Hebrew Bible proved its usefulness in every epoch and culture, for people belonging to every racial or social group. Indeed, here is sketched the possibility for every member of human society "to reach the stars," acting courageously against cowardice, weakness, laziness by climbing, in ascending line, on higher and higher ranks of the scale of spiritual values.

Wellhausen's book, Prolegomena to the History of Ancient Israel, a work of almost five hundred pages with thousands of references to the Hebrew Bible shows another facet of its author. Modern research shows that his book is full of false statements, changing even the meaning of Hebrew words when he is calling them "conjectural amendments." In order to make a long story a shorter one, we have to mention that starting with the 1930s, Scandinavian critics refuted in a sound way the entire Wellhausen criticism. On the archeological front, the mortal bullet for Wellhausen came from the respected archeologist W. F. Albright, when he published his book *From Stone Age to Christianity*. For more details, the interested reader may consult Herman Wouk's book *This Is My God* (revised edition, p. 272-280, N.Y.: Pocket Books, 1974).

2.3

The Axioms of Judaism and Related Aspects

The Ten Commandments, known also under the Greek name of the Decalogue, sum up briefly the spiritual law of God, outflowing love for the Almighty, and for one's neighbor. The first four commandments summarize the principle of love to the Supreme Power (the unique parameter on which we depend) and the last six to man. We find here more attention paid to the human element than to anything else. In the present section, and in the following, we will consider some problems raised by the specified commandments in different epochs and situations, as well as the set of members of the human society which develop their daily activities in different parts of the world. In our text, we will use sometimes the name of postulates too, instead of commandments, both of them having an equivalent meaning.

For the first time in the history of mankind are traced here precise rules of conduct from an ethical and organizational point of view. The rules are concise, profound, fundamental; they are unchangeable and could not be exceeded by the social development. This is why we find concentrated here essential rules necessary for a civilized life; they constitute the foundation of the entire Judaic system.[3] The title itself seems to us to be catchy: The Ten Commandments. The scientist or the so-called modern man may call them axioms, the religious man exactly what the Hebrew Bible calls them, but this is totally insignificant. The content is absolutely unchanged for each category. The Axioms must be respected in their entirety. None of them may undergo the smallest alteration.

If, for the sake of argument, such a thing were to occur, as a consequence, a perturbation in the entire ethical system would begin and step-by-step the entire area would undergo a shake-up. We hope this is understandable, since the considered axioms constitute the basis of a system in dynamic equilibrium: the Judaic system. It remained unshaken through the millennia, despite adverse events, an unstained witness on its pedestal. Now we are going to enunciate and comment upon "the ten axioms" of the Hebrew Bible, irreducible in content and invariant in time:

1. I am the Lord your God, who brought you out of the land of Egypt, out of the land of slavery.
2. You shall have no other gods beside me. You shall not make yourself any idols in shape of anything that is in heaven above, or that is on the earth below, or that is in the water under the earth. You shall not bow down to them nor worship them; for I, the Lord your God, am a jealous God, punishing children for the sins of their fathers, down to the third and fourth generation of those who hate me, but showing kindness to the thousandth generation of those who love me and keep my commandments.

---

[3] Judaism is a consistent system of thought and belief, built up in a rational way, based on the torah "I believe because it is absurd" is completely foreign to Judaism.

3. You shall not utter the name of the Lord your God in vain; for the Lord will not hold guiltless anyone who utters his name in vain.
4. Remember the Sabbath day to keep it holy. Six days you shall labor and do all your work; but on the seventh day, which is a day of rest in honor of the Lord your God, you shall not do any work, neither you, nor your son, nor your daughter, nor your male or female servant, nor your cattle, nor the stranger who is within your gates; for in six days the Lord made the heavens, the earth, the sea, and all that they contain, and rested on the seventh day; therefore the Lord blessed the Sabbath day and hallowed it.
5. Honor your father and your mother, that you may live long in the land which the Lord your God is giving you.
6. You shall not murder.
7. You shall not commit adultery.
8. You shall not steal.
9. You shall not testify falsely against your neighbor.
10. You shall not covet your neighbor's house; You shall not covet your neighbor's wife, nor his servant, male or female, nor his ox, nor his ass, nor anything that belongs to your neighbor.

2.4

The Postulates: One–Three and the Problem of Uniqueness

According to the enunciation, it seems that the first postulate is addressed exclusively to the Jewish people, since the Children of Israel were slaves. We shall see soon it is an incorrect interpretation, since such a statement has to be judged through a penetration of its deep meaning. On the other hand, all the other commandments do not mention any people, underscoring the universal character of the Decalogue. The first postulate has mainly three important meanings.

First, it reminds us, and the entire world, about the most disgusting social system, "slavery," and because the Jews were taken out in a unique way, they are singled out. In all Jewish religious writings recited at different festivals that slavery is mentioned, the freedom of the human spirit, the morality of the human element, plays one of the most important roles in the structure of the Jewish religious system.

Second, it is trying to underscore for the entire world that exceptional occurrence, showing that the Almighty disagrees with human slavery.

Third, God is the only parameter on which the entire universe depends. Only something like that could exceed human beings, countries, nature (since slavery was considered for a time a normal state of affairs, something similar to a natural law). Only such a parameter could develop and exert such a tremendous force on one of the most powerful kings of that time, allowing the Israelites to leave in freedom without any military intervention. Never had such an occurrence had taken place in the entire history of mankind. Well-organ-

ized groups of fighters during antiquity tried to gain freedom, but they never succeeded.

The second postulate established the interdiction regarding other gods. Here appears for the first time, in an explicit way, the aspect of uniqueness. This postulate has far-reaching objectives. Here is written clearly, explicitly, the interdiction for the human element to venerate any artifact or any other material thing. It is an order for each individual to maintain his spiritual freedom. Any discovery made by the human element, on the scale of generations, is not allowed to become a fetish. To clarify in the best possible way, there are indications where such things may eventually be found, or observed. There is only one unique interaction, one invisible parameter that acts everywhere on our Earth, on our solar system, on our galaxy, on the metagalaxy.[4]

Perhaps some individuals with a certain intellectual background are tempted to challenge such a statement. For them and for those who haven't the background to engage in a discussion of some invariant elements of our world, but who, in principle, are ready always to contradict the evidence itself, we write the following explanation. For the sake of argument, let us suppose that a unique parameter able to direct the organic and inorganic world doesn't exist. In such a case, different interactions would superpose each other. Such an interference would make difficult, if not impossible, to grasp the order that exists in the natural world. The existence of such a possibility would put under a big question mark how general laws can emerge in the domain called natural sciences. Following such a trend we may reach a negation of the human experience, and be guided toward the level of understanding of pagan antiquity, when every idol had a defined sector of activity where

---

[4] By metagalaxy, we understand that part of the Universe that can be detected now, using modern technology. This part is made up of, roughly speaking, 100 billion galaxies.

he/she was powerful. As we know, those idols (gods) fought each other, and each one could penetrate the domain of another, taking over the governance of the "fresh" conquered territory. From an ethical, scientific and religious point of view, the discovery made of the existence of an invisible, omnipresent unique parameter constitutes on a historical plan the greatest discovery of the human spirit, unequaled to this very day.

This revolutionary concept has thrown the human mind into the abstract world of thinking and, as we know today, without such a way adopted by the human mind, we would risk remaining for a very long time on very low scale of development. This helped some of us to become modern laymen which call the behavior of nature in a certain domain natural law. But if we look to the immensity of the universe and how it works, we have the feeling that a "blueprint" has been used by a Creator to determine how the universe will evolve. That discovery, made by our ancestor Abraham, has been for man the starting point in the process of conquering the terrestrial and extraterrestrial world. According to archeological discoveries, the historical distance between Abraham and Moses was more than one thousand years.[5]

The third postulate is an impulse given to the human element to look for the unknown, to do research. At the same time, the postulate tries to polarize the attention about the danger of not performing a careful analysis of the results obtained from doing research. Indeed, it is mentioned with great clarity: God will not hold guiltless anyone who utters his name in vain. The entire material world is conducted according to certain laws which cannot be ignored; if you do it so, you will be condemned by your fellow citizens as well as by posterity that cannot, and will not, forgive your behavior. Any conclusions that do not fit

---

[5] See "Science Digest" Special Edition, Winter 1979, page 30.

into the unchangeable laws of nature, directed in a unique way, must vanish.

But the only proof that we have dwelled for a while on the surface of our planet will consist in our contribution brought to the field of knowledge, making easier the life of the human species, so that those who follow may benefit from our gathering. It is quite possible that an individual will pass away before the correctness of his work is recorded. In that case, his followers, directly related, or those influenced by him or his facts, will get the right payment in time. We don't go into details. The problem can be pushed ahead on the scale of generations.

Before we start the next section we would like to reemphasize some aspects regarding the postulates. According to postulate one, through perseverance even the most disgusting social system known to man can be removed. The second postulate opens the door to the entire universe where the human mind may make tremendous discoveries. But nowhere will he be able to discover the residence of the unique interaction, because that interaction is present everywhere but it is invisible and untouchable. Only naive thinking, connected to a concrete image in the mind of some individuals, makes them believe that the residence of the unique God exists somewhere, at very great distance.

Since every human being is born with sensory organs, he/she can detect occurrences in the surroundings. That complex process, in time, opens new vistas of knowledge. Some individuals develop the ability to find different methods in a completely unexpected way. When, in the boiling new era, different branches of human knowledge are connected via higher mathematics, the mind may recall suddenly the abstract spirit used thousands of years ago by the Hebrew Bible. The human mind was trained at the fire of knowledge in deep antiquity, and this had a positive contribution to develop abstract mathematics, the "concrete" main carrier in the field of strong science.[6]

This impressive progress and some observations made in biology and related fields made some individuals emit the utterance: "the function creates the organ." If this is true, it means that any being possessing a superior structure may reach the same stage as a human being. As has been proved, this is not possible; therefore, the statement is false. Nobody has ever gotten from a monkey even the slightest indication that such a thing will occur, at least according to the best of our knowledge. As we know, function may develop a certain existing organ. The lack of use, in time, may make the organ remain in an undeveloped stage. Practice confirms our point of view. The intestinal appendix, as well as the wisdom teeth, are considered rudiments of the primitive man. But how does the creation of a new organ begin? Usually literary explanations are involved, since nobody, up to now, has been able to pack the facts into a severe mathematical language, or to bring in some empirical facts in order to determine this. We cannot, and we may not, make any extrapolations that can guide to false conclusions.

Some scientists accused religion, in general, as being a hindrance to research, discovery, and interpretation of the empirical data. Most likely, those researchers knew religion as taught by a priest in the spirit of concrete images, made up in a naive way; that kind of teaching is completely forbidden by the basic abstract spirit of the Hebrew Bible. The concrete detected by the sensory organs pushed them over the ten basic axioms, unique in their essence for the entire mankind. Thus, the phenomenon of departure of the individual from the immutable,

---

6 By "Strong Science" we understand Physics, for eg., where using mathematics, we are able to calculate and predict in a quantitive way, some occurrences. The other branches, like psychology, medicine, we call them by benevolence "Soft Science."

established trajectory had taken place when the straight line has been transformed in a broken one.

Therefore, in the light of contemporary scientific discoveries, the optics of the individual understanding undergoes some changes. The images formed at different moments of one's life are modifying their contour under the pressure of more facts added to the known reality. A person without a background in a domain that develops, may find himself at a certain moment frustrated, I would dare to say, even robbed, of his most precious images. I couldn't say that even the scientist feels comfortable in such moments, but he/she passes over such a loss more easily, being absorbed, at least partially, by new discoveries, the necessity to imagine new devices, or to elaborate hypotheses to explain a new phenomenon. In other words, parallel with the work performed, he/she takes over another role: that of a creator. The special feeling given by some new findings opens an unknown door in his psychological structure and it helps him to pass over the losses connected to the field of religion. However, from time to time, doubts, a lot of doubts, return to his ever-searching mind. But he keeps working and, step-by-step, finding; sometimes, deeply absorbed by daily tasks, forgetting everything, until a special event may "push him back" to his initial status.

2.5

The Postulates: Four–Five, and the Material World

We are going to analyze the next two axioms, or postulates. The fourth is closely connected with the third; it has its own clear distinction, claiming in a peremptory way, the necessity for restfulness. Without rest, the possibilities for an individual to make any effort, on physical or intellectual ground, approach zero. Without rest, the creative capabilities of each individual are diminished, and finally the consequences are critical, since nothing can compensate for rest of the human muscles and brain.

This postulate doesn't require only the seventh day as an obligatory day of rest, it also requires that any living being belonging to your house must be a beneficiary of this commandment; and once in seven years, even the land used for agriculture must remain unused. The scientific content of this postulate started to be appreciated in our era. As it is well known, the seventh year is called a sabbatical year, its action being extended to other domains of human activity. The modern human being, seeing what restfulness means, tried to extend the sphere of action of this postulate. The extension contains no contradiction with the mentioned postulate, since the Decalogue in ensemble gives the elements necessary to organize a stable, viable society in which all bipedals living, will deserve to be called human beings.

The fifth postulate raises a problem of elementary ethics, with profound implications for the entire society. It is built up in such a way that when it is translated in the language of the exact sciences, the enunciation would be: "if. . ., then." If you will give the required respect to your parents, those who brought you to life, who took care of you when you were growing up, then you, human creature, will enjoy a corresponding life on the planet given to you by the Originator. A life of good relations gives you peace of mind, and as a consequence, an increase of longevity that will allow you to enjoy your life and everything that belongs to you. The desire of any parent is to have gifted children, behaving correctly and respecting the moral norms of the society. Hence, to respect those norms means to respect your parents and primarily, the Maker of mankind, the unique Parent, whose desire is to build up and maintain a civilized society where brotherhood and understanding are the predominant factors.

Before we close this section, we would like to emphasize the fact that in the Hebrew Bible, no names are mentioned for the days of the week. To distinguish the weekdays from one another, they are mentioned as the first day, the second day, etc.; but for the seventh day, the name of Sabbath has been chosen; that means rest, to underscore its special significance for the entire society. Taking into account the simple fact that it includes any being belonging to one's house, it appears to be an order given to the human race about how to enjoy the precious gift called freedom.

Therefore, on Mount Sinai Moses didn't have only the revelation concerning the Decalogue, he was also taught the meaning of freedom that must be made possible for the entire human society. We cannot find in existing religious systems any indication showing the slightest hint or concern for the human element and his place in the social structure as a free man. In Judaism, such a requirement is done with great care showing the necessity for human freedom, considering it a main concern since without it, no happiness is possible for the human element, or for society as a whole.

2.6

The Postulates: Six-Eight and the Human Society

The next three postulates are called, by some critics of the Hebrew Bible, negative, since we find here clear, blunt statements regarding interdictions, just as in the case of the second and third postulates. Then we may see that the axioms of Judaism, list three do's and seven don'ts. The seven don'ts leave little doubt as to what one is not supposed to do. Fencing in only the negative, an open file for the positive remains. Therefore, far from being a bad thing, as the critics like to suggest, we can see the positive aspect of such a predominant negative aspect. We will comment further after we present all ten axioms.

We consider these three postulates together, since they have, in a way, something in common: a direct assault (according to some critics) on the fellow human. The first one pertains directly to his life, the second one to his wife, and the third one to his property. There is a very close connection between these postulates and the previous five, and they regard the life of each member of humanity. If the postulates are respected, an honest life for the individual and the entire society will result.

The axiomatic foundation of the Jewish law doesn't make any departure of the individual from practice. On the contrary, we can see here the existence of an ethical potential which in a very real sense maintains a continuous freshness of these rules on the scale of indefinite time, giving us the possibility of discovering new valences embedded in these "old" and everlastingly young axioms.

Here we want to recall two postulates: five, belonging to the previous section and seven, considered in this section. These two postulates try to persuade the human elements to pay attention to the fact that a society with profligate elements will not fulfill the postulate five, and such a life of lust will not bring anything good to an individual, to his parents, or to the society where one lives. Finally, such an element will not spend too many days on the surface of the earth created for him to enjoy. The infection with HIV[7] that we are witnessing in our day is, unfortunately, a strong example of what such elements may do for their fellows, and themselves. They became a danger for the entire society. It isn't too difficult for anyone to understand the consequences for their offspring.

---

[7] Human immunodeficiency virus, which may cause AIDS.

2.7

The Postulates: Nine-Ten and the Social Context?

The human social element has undergone an evolution in this world along its historical path. Living conditions have changed. He became closer to his fellow man and even to some things or other beings, that started to be a part of his daily life. His psychological feelings started to be more selective. The closeness between fellows of different sex started to undergo changes too. At the very beginning, it was the simple physical attraction, the only purpose being to perpetuate the species. In the process of cohabitation, their characters were polished from generation to generation and feelings for one another underwent an evolution. The human sentiments increased in intensity, and they started to take care of each other.

If we try to analyze how the sentiment of property has developed among humans, we may say that its birth took place on a sentimental ground, other aspects came into the equation of economics later. Once the feeling of property developed, regulations were needed to determine in which way something may belong to one individual or to another. There are known legislations elaborated on different stages of development of the human society. For instance, in a society based on slavery, the owner of a slave had the right to do whatever he liked with his slave, even to kill him. The entire life of a slave was at the owner's discretion.

In such a moment of evolution of the human collective organization, the Decalogue was given, which takes into account the existing state of affairs and moves forward in an ascending line. For example, the ninth postulate doesn't make any distinction of social rank. Everything is on equal footing and the only standard used is the human social element and how he has to deal with the other members of the human collectivity, which we may call the human social body. To testify falsely against another fellow is considered an injustice. Since such a behavior cannot be tolerated, a countermeasure has to be taken. What differs from one epoch to another are the punishments. This is why they are not, and cannot, remain invariant.

The last postulate, like the other, deals with human beings, their life, the love among them as they organize themselves over centuries and millennia. These are the celebrated axioms known by the entire world under the name: The Ten Commandments.

2.8

The Ten Commandments and the Epoch

As we mentioned in the previous section, the state of affairs in certain surroundings cannot be neglected. We humans live in a society and some reciprocal influences take place, on one hand. On the other hand, it is almost impossible to change everything by one stroke. This is why we want to insist here on such aspects. The Decalogue possesses a uniqueness which makes its application most relevant to Israel's universal priestly mission. The prohibition of worshipping nature, the making of "graven images," establishes rigorously the distinctive character of Israel's monotheism, which marks it off with sharp definition from all other forms of god-belief.

The Sinaitic Covenant has a twofold implication: universal and national. The Jewish religious system based on the Decalogue is charged with a moral dynamism capable of transforming the individual and, through the individual, the entire society, where his family constitutes a brick in the great building of that civilized organization. The observance of the commandments and the laws derived from them is no longer a mere isolated act. Insofar as it contributes to the individual's moral stability, and affects his general conduct, it becomes a social act. What can be more eloquent than the law of love formulated in the "Golden Rule": "Thou shalt love thy fellow as thyself" (Leviticus 19:18). It is easy to see that this is expressed in a general way to include the non-Israelite as well, and it has obviously a universal resonance. Since we discuss here the invariant rules which are true axioms of mankind, we must go back to some other ancient codes frequently quoted: the Hammurabi and Hittite codes. In both cases, the motive invoked is the protection of property; in the Torah, based on the Decalogue, the motive is the protection of personality. Even the slave had rights of a free man and was never recognized as an absolute possession of the owner. If he ran away, it was forbidden to deliver him back to his master (Deuteronomy 23:16-17). The Hammurabi Code imposed the death penalty on those who aided runaway slaves. (Other aspects regarding Hammurabi's code and other legislations of antiquity will be given in chapter five.) The slightest injury to the body of a slave gave him his freedom (Exodus 21:26-27).

Slavery was a law imposed by the epoch due to the level of production of material goods, but Judaism couldn't accept it. The disagreement with slavery prepared the way of freedom for all mankind. The slaves of the Jewish society had so many rights that the owner himself had to try to get rid of them. The Torah doesn't admit any distinction between king and noble, commoner and slave, native and stranger, other than those of social function, all being equal in the eyes of the law.

Postulate four tells us about the Sabbath as our day of rest. The Babylonians, too, had their day of rest called Shappatu. But while the Babylonian day of rest was a day of danger, the quality of holiness ascribed to the Sabbath made it a day of moral and spiritual regeneration, and thereby a day "blessed of the Lord" (Exodus 20:11). The same is true of the other three festivals: the Feast of Unleavened Bread, Pentecost, and the Tabernacles. All of them are ascribed as holy convocations, in contrast to the harvest festivals of the Canaanites, which were marked by obscene rites and orgiastic scenes. The Jewish New Year, with which the Day of Atonement is closely connected, is also described as a holy convocation, to distinguish it sharply from the Canaanite New Year, in which the Tamuz ritual of a dying god formed the central feature of the entire celebration.

God's love for the stranger is exemplified in the previous mentioned command to love the stranger (Deut. 10:18, 19). In this law is revealed the universal love of God. The fact that Israel has been chosen doesn't limit his love for the human race. Israel has the distinction of being the peculiar people through whom God has revealed his love for all mankind. Using the concept of set introduced toward the end of the first chapter, we may say that Israel is apart from the sets of the world's social elements, and yet it remains a part of it, being in fact a particular subset of the general set of social elements because it has a special mission in the world. This mission has been entrusted to the Children of Israel who, after centuries of Egyptian bondage, had escaped from a hostile environment of sophisticated vice at the top of that society, and a brutish undescribable degradation at the bottom.

It should be clear to everyone that it was not Israel's mission in the past, nor is it in the present, to convert everyone to the Jewish religion. The significance of the covenant promulgated at Sinai marked the historical moment when Israel became a united nation having as a common ground the ten axioms enforced by the Torah and its national career pledged in consecration to serve the unique universal God of all humanity. The unique interaction, due to which the entire machinery of the universe is in motion, as we should see, acts in a way to help and please the social human element. It tries to satisfy man's necessities, to make his environment more agreeable, to give him satisfaction for his positive deeds. The social elements are directed toward friendly relationships among people, each one having the right to life, love, and happiness.

We can see the lack of any special promise for some time in

the future. What the Decalogue promulgates is equality before the law for all human beings. The epoch when the axioms were given, as well as their content, exceed any human possibility, any human mind, and that is why they are entitled by the singular statement: divine law. We have to recognize that an atheist may argue about all our statements, saying that more than two thousand years ago some philosophers reached a very high level of generalization, and some of them are studied even in our days. That is true, but none of them was able to understand the evolution of the human society or the future structure of that society, and moreover, they were incapable of imagining how a society without slavery would look like (see 5.3). In the next chapter, we will see why the eventual objections raised by the hypothetical atheist cannot be taken seriously, and that the mentioned name is a proper one for the ten axioms of the Hebrew Bible.

2.9

Points of View

There is a coincidence between the beginning of the civilized world and the effort made by man to improve his existence. During that time, man developed his intellectual power that pushed him along his entire existence to continuously enriching his life. The human practical activity was influenced by the achievements obtained on a spiritual level. Step-by-step, man became the owner of a treasure: the knowledge of the laws that govern the material world.

When the Newtonian Theory was flourishing, some west European youth became extremely confident about their unlimited possibilities to explain the behavior of the material world. They were convinced that nothing could be a hindrance in their way to learn everything about the past and future of the universe. All the extrapolations made at that time appear now as naive ways applied to a very complicated universe. The so-called mechanistically determined universe was a total failure. Their entire point of view has been buried by the world's scientific working teams. Each one worked in its domain, floating on the agitated sea of science. Each one considered that modern man had enough knowledge to guide himself in such a world, since according to general belief, the philosophical attitude of an epoch is determined by its cultural background.

Practice did not confirm that belief. The ethical aspect was completely neglected. The invariance of some norms established in antiquity and contained in the Hebrew Bible were completely forgotten, although, basically, they were adopted by the Christian religion with some modifications. The events developed before World War II and during that war show clearly the "elevated moral" and conscience of some states, foremost among them being Hitler's Germany. On the other hand, a great social experiment took place in Russia during seventy bitter years of human life, that tried to replace the invariant elements of the Hebrew Bible through other "moral elements" of atheistic nature. Surely, everyone knows the result. None of the ethical norms of the Decalogue could be refuted among the borders of that atheistic state. Practice forced them to adopt, without any changes, the postulates:

- Six (You shall not murder).
- Seven (You shall not commit adultery).
- Eight (You shall not steal).

Hitler denied everything that was Jewish except some precious Jewish creations, Jewish property, etc., which was stolen from the Jewish owners and transformed into "pure Aryan goods." He built up a society where all those postulates were abolished. To kill was permitted by law. For example, one of his highly ranked ministers said "when I am talking about culture, I have the feeling I have to start firing my handgun." Therefore, negation of the axioms of the Hebrew Bible is quite possible, but using them in the construction of a society reverses the wheel of history, pulling back the entire human community that is on the threshold of barbarian cruelty. According to multiple complex relations between the social elements and nature, a reciprocal influence takes place. In the same manner, but on another scale, a society is influencing its inhabitants through its moral norms, adopted and applied in everyday life. Those elements who swim, in sense, with the moral flow of that society will undergo a corresponding change of shape in the ethical field and, in the same sense, they will influence that society as well as its future development. The previously discussed cases constitute an experimental confirmation of this point of view.

2.10

The Individual and the Human Society

The specificity of contemporary man consists, among other concerns, in the fact that his connection to life raises many questions and constitutes for him a major preoccupation. He tries to comprehend known and unknown facts and to synthesize them, in order to express the result in a concise form. Some exponents of the exact sciences, generally without sufficient knowledge of the Hebrew Bible (sometimes the knowledge in this field approaches zero), being preoccupied with special problems belonging to their profession, envision a chasm between science and the Hebrew Bible. Those scientists are in the best case "intellectual workers" who, in certain moments of their lives, were in contact with people from whom they heard some interpretations which have nothing in common with the Hebrew Bible.

For instance, the statement, the human element may consider himself a central figure in the universe, made some clergymen forget their background, start giving solutions in problems of celestial mechanics. Those gentlemen placed themselves in a frame of reference in which they did not belong and, forgetting their mission, tried to convince even the Jewish people that these clergymen are the true successors of Moses, propagating the true faith. The well-known medieval disputes, when all expenses had to be paid by the Jewish communities, had as a final purpose to force the Jews to give up their religion. If those prelates didn't understand the essence of Christianity whose roots are grounded in the Jewish soil of the Hebrew Bible, how could they see and read the statements regarding love, righteousness for all social elements, used by the Christian church? They stepped down from their pulpit of apostles and became chieftains of cults, military commanders, etc. How could they apply in a correct way what had been taken out of the Hebrew Bible and put into another context?

Their new position was incompatible with their mission to propagate love and understanding. Those official exponents of the Christian creed forgot completely the Hebrew Bible's allegory: All human beings have common parents, Adam and Eve. This potential function of the Hebrew Bible was taken out and rewritten in an explicit way by Christianity under the statement, all human beings are brothers. The Axioms of Judaism take into account the fact that the humans may lose sight of the fact that, in time, relatives become more distant. For example, brothers are called those born from common parents, but only the first generation. Among a group of families having a common ancestry, the distance is increased from generation to generation. The closeness of the members of a social body is underlined by their common origin, and this means that none of them is entitled to privileges, or to transform his fellow man into a subordinate.

The genealogy given by the Hebrew Bible is valid for any society, it doesn't matter whether it just emerged from the barbarian stage or is a well-developed one. We do not ask anybody to take our written words for granted. Man's mission on Earth is to be armed with knowledge, since only then will he be able to act in a conscious way in the process of creation, at a level of unspecified scales. Therefore, any kind of creation cannot be against the Jewish religion; it can always be inscribed on the curve of behavior of any believer. The realizations obtained as a result of research, open the door to a better understanding of reality in order to improve the life of the human species, the main aim written on the frontispiece of Jewish thought, according to the Book of Books.

The so-called contradictions between the Jewish religion and modern society, commented upon by some visionaries belonging to different currents of modern thought, are based on erroneous interpretations and by lack of knowledge. It doesn't matter who made them: representatives of a religious branch, atheists, or scientists. Their position has nothing to do with the fundamental axioms of Judaism. The Decalogue is an irreducible synthesis of human conscience, and we may say that the phenomenon of its appearance coincides with the birth of that conscience. This is why the religious man is considered to be of divine origin; the atheist admits the existence of that synthesis and maintains that it has a historical nature, but still he cannot see its invariance. Usually, he would rather quote Karl Marx's statement, "What has a historical character, i.e., came up in a certain moment of social development, has to vanish in another moment of social growth." Marx was not a scientist and his knowledge in Jewish thought was almost nonexistent, even though he was of Jewish descent. His statements about Judaism are completely insignificant, and it can easily be seen, he was rather a dilettante in Jewish affairs.

In the next chapter, we are going to consider scientific proofs regarding the Hebrew Bible and we would like to underline in advance why we are so sure about the unchangeable value of Jewish teaching based on the Book of Books. In the first chapter, we mentioned that in the exact sciences there are the so-called invariants. Today their use is unanimously accepted as being of great importance. For instance in physics, to establish the invariance of some relations when we pass from one system of reference to another constitutes a proof of their independence of the system of coordinates where the experiment took place, or where they were obtained. Their validity is conserved. We cannot have physical laws which are valid only in privileged systems of reference.

In any decent human society, in the over three thousand years since the Decalogue was given, those laws have remained unchanged (invariant). Different societies may be assimilated with frames of reference about what actually they are and so, step-by-step, we get a permanent freshness of the axioms in human history. To conserve the essence of the Book of Books as an exclusive property of the Jewish people, a testament and proof of their golden ethics and to which territory on the surface of the earth they are entitled, constitutes a duty of honor for any civilized nation. To keep their Torah, the Jews travelled like phantoms from country to country, and not rarely were persecuted, misunderstood, and sometimes killed by those who had the duty and honor to be their best friends and even defenders.[8]

Last, and not least, from a historical point of view, the Decalogue is the first system that is given in an axiomatic way. Its quintessence being the human element and his life, in a social context regardless of the society to which he belongs or his social position. Taken as a unique indivisible block, it represents a universal guiding principle for the physical social

---

[8] The Christian version of the Decalogue contains the modified axiom that mentions the people of Israel and changing the day of rest to Sunday. The other postulates, like 6, 7, 8, and 9, where taken unchanged. Appendix A contains the Christian version of the Decalogue.

body, and may be compared with the guiding principle of the nonexistence of a perpetuum mobile of first and second kind used in the branch of physics called thermodynamics.[9]

[9] The laws of nature are such that it is ,possible to construct a perpetuum mobile (of the first kind). The first kind refers to the law of conservation energy, which means that you need a source of energy in order to get mechanical work. The second kind refers to the impossibility of obtaining an engine that works using one source of heat only. For example, using a very hot block of iron in order to get mechanical work you need steam, and that can be obtained using a cold reservoir, too.

Three

The Hebrew Bible is using the concrete-particular to support abstract ideas, and is employing the abstract to assemble social concrete items.

— Anonymous

Chapter 3

Scientific Facts and the Hebrew Bible

3.1

Introduction

We are going to analyze here events from the past, written for the future (sections 3.1-3.5). That past is filled with dreams and thoughts kept alive by fragments of memory. All those past experiences, rich and poor, wait patiently to be summoned from deep slumber. When that information percolates through the researcher's mind, the past may start to resonate with his deepest feelings. Using that information via a scientific analysis, it is flabbergasting how some branches of knowledge may open anyone's eyes, discovering for interested people, a new world.

Since for us, science is the art of the soluble, comforting humans by dispelling the unknown, we hope that at the end of the present chapter, the reader will be able to glimpse the immensity of the machinery of the universe, and using the corresponding information, he may get a rational understanding of what some say is nothing else than pure belief. But this is only one side of the coin; the other side will give him the needed background to measure the huge step made by Moses when he freed his brothers from bondage and how that act, together with his entire work, constitutes a unique giant step for all mankind (sections 3.6-3.14).

3.2

The Decalogue and the Human Being

As we mentioned in the previous chapter, the Decalogue possesses a unique universality and since Israel is its carrier in original form (the unique obliged carrier), he is in the position of having a universal priestly mission. The rules of conduct it prescribes are sufficiently comprehensive to constitute primary requirements for every social body, at any epoch. It forbids the deification of nature, including the sun, the moon, and the stars, as well as the making of graven images. The prohibition against worshipping nature and its correlatives marks the distinctive character of Israel's monotheism.

Sometimes different writings suggest that the Decalogue, or a part of it, is not as unique as was thought. Usually

Hammurabi's Law is the strongest example. What we would like to emphasize here again is that Hammurabi and other rulers of that time launched laws with a common denominator: their epoch. In no other code is piety found as an obligation, moral conduct as a duty, or the prohibition of lust and covetous desires. Their laws didn't contain that fundamental ferment that makes the Decalogue unchangeable in time, a necessary and sufficient ingredient to ensure the conservation of its nonperishable content. This special distinct quality, which unites the invariance with its content, gives the Decalogue its universal validity.

The substance and scope of Israel's mission is indicated here, whilst other specific duties and obligations were developed in Moses' books, where the Decalogue became incorporated. Those books have twofold implications: national and universal.

- *National, since when the Israelites arrived at Sinai, in the third month of their departure from Egypt, the Sinaitic covenant between them and the universal God, the unique regulator of the world's interactions, took place.*
- *Universal, since here were given the Ten Commandments, which contain fundamental elementary principles applicable in any epoch, to any society.*

Here, for the first time in history, the human element received recognition of his capacity, regardless of the social stratum to which he belonged, as well as the needed impulse to be launched with confidence on the curve of creation. Here was established full social equality before the unique supreme power that created the world. Since God created man, too, man has to do the same thing: to procreate and to develop the created world. This means that more than three thousand years ago, the limitless power of creativity was stimulated by the Sinaitic covenant, guiding the people who had just been liberated from slavery to use the power that resides in their minds and bodies.

We suppose that it is more than relevant that the Jewish religious concept is charged, from its birth, with a moral dynamism capable of transforming the individual and, through the individual, society. It is enough to mention the statement," Adam, I gave you the world, you have to know it and to perfect it; the world which I created has to be finished and you have to do it." Through the covenant of Sinai, Israel has to be apart from the world and yet remain a part of it. This means that while keeping distinct from the surrounding nations, Israel was to throw its effort into the current flow of civilizations, seeking to raise human life and human understanding to higher levels.

Another facet of the covenant of Sinai is that it shows Israel as a small subset making a new beginning, on a national level, in its Promised Land. In the meantime, Israel has to serve the unique God, as well as all humanity, as part of the universal duty of its priestly mission.[1]

---

[1] See the scheme regarding the genealogy of all people scattered over the entire terra, given in the next chapter.

3.3

The Decalogue and the Jewish Daily Life

We want to show briefly how the wise men of Israel succeeded in applying the axioms of Judaism, in a creative way, to the daily life of the individual and to governing the entire nation. About three thousand years ago, the Philistines, warriors from Crete of Greek descent, landed on a narrow southern coastal belt, which they conquered, burning local towns. Because of their new techniques introduced on the battlefield, they presented a danger for the entire country. Then the clamor for a king invested with supreme power became stronger and stronger. The existing judge (I Samuel 8:5) opposed the demand, fearing that such a king might become a tyrant over the people. Finally he yielded, but only after a constitution in contemporary language, was approved which defined the royal rights and strictly delimited the royal powers.

Thus Samuel, after Abraham and Moses, gained credit for one of the greatest contributions ever made to the political thought of man. Here we can see a direct relationship between the axioms of Judaism and a truly democratic way that determines the relation between the governor and those who are governed.[2] As we know, the king chosen was Saul, and due to the mentioned law he has to be regarded the first

---

2 T.H. Robinson Palestine in General History (Scheweich Lecture, 1929, p.44.

constitutional king in history (1025 B.C.). Saul embodied this truly Magna Carta in a book that he placed before YAHVE[3] for the guidance of future kings of Israel (I Samuel 10:25).

After him was chosen David (1012-972 B.C.), and he followed the same golden rule required by the constitution. He attached to his royal court advisors in the persons of leading prophets like Gad and Nathan, who did not hesitate to rebuke the king for his wrongdoings and even constrain him to follow the right way. If we look back in history and see the great authority that King David had, his military successes, his great achievements in uniting the country, etc., perhaps we can realize the great importance of the constitution in limiting the king's power, daring to criticize him, and to show him the way to follow.

---

[3] YHVH, Tetragram of the Lord's name; not to be spoken. The word Yahve, used in our day, has the same meaning.

3.4

Abstract Concepts and Correct Results

Judaism and its entire system rests on two basic doctrines:

1. The belief in only one God, introduced in an axiomatic way, which from a scientific point of view means that the entire universe depends on only one parameter.

2. The election of Israel, the chosen people, to be the bearers of this belief.

The only God recognized by Israel, to whom it owes absolute homage, is the living God whose creative energy has been at work in every part of the universe since the moment the world and man were brought into existence. A problem debated by philosophers and some scientists preoccupied by religion, as friends or enemies, is whether the world came into being out of nothing, or out of preexistent matter. What Judaism specifies in its doctrine of creation is that the entire universe is not a product of chance, but is governed by well-defined laws. Therefore, we may say it is a blueprint of the Almighty (a superhuman power).

According to Jewish belief, God is not identical with the world nor limited by it. For instance, a Talmudic sentence expressing the divine transcendence says: "He is the Place of the World, but the world is not His Place." This rule is out of any pantheistic interpretation that would identify God with nature.[4] The only parameter on which the universe depends cannot be touched or seen as the pagan ancestors tried to do when they worshiped idols, the wind, or a celestial object. They had to feel or see the presence of something to believe in.

As we noticed in the first chapter, the world of science has to deal with abstract things, which in turn give very real effects. In other words, the Hebrew Bible's structure is similar to the scientific approach. Each chapter, each conclusion of a solved problem, must be in accord with the axioms of Judaism. As is well known, any work belonging to the foundation of a branch of science, from a modern point of view, is set up in such a way. How could the Hebrews acquire that amount of knowledge and take out the essence of it in a synthesized manner? This is the great mystery which no school of philosophy can answer, nor any branch of contemporary science.

---

4 Even Spinoza was less pantheistic than some philosophers considered. He said that God's presence can be seen in everything around us. Indeed, according to his demonstrations, the entire matter is governed by the same laws, but he did not identify God with matter itself.

3.5

Strong Science and Two of the Jewish Festivals

We are going to present, beside the basic fact of invariance, six other proofs based on pure science, impossible to explain in a rational way. The first one is in regard to the number of people who came to Egypt (72; Jacob and his family, according to the recorded data of the Hebrew Bible), and the number of people leaving Egypt (600,000) after 400 years of slavery. Our estimation of the latter is based on the Malthusian Law and the period of time needed for a population to be doubled. This occasion is commemorated at Passover, when the Israelites left Egypt as free men. Moses, the giant fighter for freedom, succeeded in making that grand step, to pass over the threshold of slavery by destroying for his people the fence, or rather the thick wall, that separated them from being free. Passover is also considered the birth of the Jewish people, although there is material proof that Abraham lived approximately 1,300 years earlier, but our people did not become united under the same law until Moses freed them from Egyptian slavery and gave them the law needed to live together and to conduct the daily affairs of a gregarious people.

The second festival is known as Shavuot, sometimes called the Feast of Weeks, or Pentecost, a Greek word that means the fiftieth day, since the holiday comes seven weeks after Passover, or the fiftieth day after the first festival. The Jews received on that day the axioms that constitute a true tool of control and of conduct in every action of daily life. Therefore, just as Passover is the birthday of the Jewish people, so Shavuot is the birthday of the Jewish axiomatic foundation of religion and, of course, the Jewish law of international resonance. The nineteenth and twentieth chapters of the book of Exodus describe those moments, when amid thunder, lightning, and the blasts of the shofar, Moses revealed the law to our forefathers. Then, by embracing the Torah, a disorganized ignorant horde, just freed from slavery, became a consecrated people.

As we can see, liberty and law, religion and righteousness, go hand in hand, with the Jewish people and its history being intermingled. We may conclude that Shavuot concludes what Passover started: Since it isn't enough to be free, you must have certain, precise rules of how to act in different situations, how to understand different necessities as a free man. It is not enough just to believe what is right; you must do what is right.

3.6

The Fourth Axiom and Strong Science

The second proof that shows a new glimpse of light on the Hebrew Bible is connected with rather a completely unexpected branch of strong science: physics. If we consider a closed furnace and we look into a small aperture made in such a way that no light can penetrate from outside, we see nothing if the temperature is below 500°C. We may sense heat and, using suitable thermal measuring devices, we may measure the thermal radiation and eventually its spectral distribution, but it is not until the temperature gets higher than 500°C, that we begin to see light. The first color will be red 600°C – 1000°C, then as the temperature rises, it changes to orange 1100°C, yellow 1200°C, and then to nearly white 1400°C. What we will see in the furnace depends on the temperature only and is independent of the materials of which the furnace is constructed. The energy radiated from such a small aperture in a furnace is of an electromagnetic nature and it is called "black-body" radiation, because a black surface is one which absorbs all the energy that falls on it.

Sometimes the term "cavity of radiation" also is used. A small opening in a large cavity may be thought of as a trap that lets in any energy that strikes it and, being small, makes it difficult for the considered energy to leave the cavity again. Therefore, the hole of the cavity absorbs essentially all the energy that falls on it from outside. That which does get out is then emitted as by a "black body," and is representative of the properties of the radiation belonging to the inside cavity. The absorption and emission of the radiation takes place in small, discrete amounts, called quanta.

Electromagnetic energy is transmitted via electromagnetic waves. Such a wave has the remarkable property of not needing any medium to propagate. It can be transmitted even in a vacuum. A mathematical relation, based on a physical law called Planck's Law of Radiation, shows that for such a cavity, the radiation may take place for certain discrete values of a parameter n: The radiation takes place for $n = 1$, $n = 2$, $n = 3$, $n = 4$, $n = 5$, $n = 6$. For $n = 7$, no radiation will occur. It behaves as though nature were at rest.

Work six days per week and the seventh day will be your day for rest (see Axiom 4, section 2.3). Often we find in the critical literature of the Hebrew Bible and Jewish customs, a statement regarding the number seven, saying that it plays an important role in the Jewish religious system. As we noticed earlier, the Jewish religious system is strictly monotheistic, and all customs used in this system are based on the Torah. But we must say that we have doubts about the fact that any individual more than three thousand years ago knew quantum mechanics, a branch of physics that deals with the quanta mentioned above. This is the second example of the impossibility of any human to have known, in deep antiquity, facts discovered between 1900 and 1925. This extra-human knowledge has to be attributed to the elaboration of the Ten Commandments too. The concept of invariance was introduced in 1905, therefore also at the beginning of the twentieth century.

---

[5] N.J. Ionescu-Pallas, Private communication..

Some readers may find our presentation based on strong science merely a coincidence, not necessarily a proof. Our research in this field started from a Jewish religious story based on the Hebrew Bible, and this is the obtained result. Of course, everybody is free to believe whatever he wants.

3.7

A Question and Its Answer

The third proof regarding the Hebrew Bible is based on pure scientific research. The Russian writer Dostoyevsky, in his well-known novel *The Brothers Karamazov,* shows the preoccupation of humans regarding the origin of our universe and the so-called contradiction of the facts described in the Hebrew Bible and reality. He presents a certain man called Smerdyakov who asked a servant of Karamazov's house, Grigory, the following question:

"The Maker created light on the first day and the Sun, the Moon, and the Stars on the fourth. But where did the light shine from on the first day?" For his curiosity he was beaten up. Therefore, the problem raised here has a certain logic, and at first look, it seems insoluble. In other words, the contradiction is evident.

Indeed, as long as our knowledge is limited to our solar system only, we may consider that what is written in Genesis as senseless. But, dear reader, please don't jump to conclusions, since modern science confirms step-by-step the basic elements of the Hebrew Bible. Indeed some theoretical scientific papers published in the 1950s showed the possibility of the presence of a radiation remnant from the beginning of our universe, in a range of five to seven Kelvins. In 1965, that radiation was detected in a experimental way by two researchers working for Bell Lab. That radiation has been identified as emanating from the moment of the creation of our universe; indeed, before any celestial body had come into being. We may say that the curiosity of Smerdyakov is now easily satisfied, and we must see that what occurred, in reality, was the curiosity of the writer himself who had doubts about that statement of the Hebrew Bible. (A new coincidence?)

The light had shone before the stars and galaxies were formed. The event that marked the beginning of our universe is known as the Big Bang, and we may call that radiation the Big Bang Light. That detectable light had heated the matter of the universe at extremely high temperatures. The temperature has decreased with the expansion of the universe and radiation, but it filled uniformly the entire universe, and that primary light still exists. Invisible to the naked eye, it can be registered by radiotelescopes, being practically the same in all directions. Recent experiments showed small deviations in uniformity which, extrapolated to the entire universe, may explain the formation of stars, galaxies, and other celestial bodies. The radiation of 2.7 K, called the relic radiation, is extremely weak. Its source is far away and the temperature is low, but it makes it possible for us humans to comprehend the content of one of the chapters of the Hebrew Bible and thus to have at least a glimpse of the extra-human dimension of the basis of the unique Book of Books, whether one is a believer or not.

3.8

Genesis Days and the World's Age

The fourth proof regards the so-called discrepancy between the age of the universe according to cosmology (between 15 and 18 billion years), and the time of creation considered by the Hebrew Bible as being six days. Nobody could watch the clock up to the sixth day when Adam appeared. It seems to be a chasm between the presented data; there is no avoiding the issue here. Indeed, the first verse of Genesis is clear: in the beginning, a primeval substance was created, and from this substance the heavens and the Earth were made during the subsequent six days. To rationalize how such an explanation is possible we must go back to the amalgamated concept of time-space.

Historically, scientists and laymen have pictured time as something like an ever-rolling stream pervading all motion and carrying the contents of the universe irresistibly from past to future. Even Isaac Newton, the great British scientist and founder of classical mechanics, supposed that time is absolute and universal, and standard clocks were supposed to agree on the rate of flow irrespective of their location or motion: on stars, planets, fast-moving spaceships, etc. As we can see, once more we are in the field of the strong science known as physics.

The appearance of Einstein's Special Theory of Relativity in 1905 brought about the total collapse of the concept of an absolute, uniform time, as well as of a universal now. Time itself became a structure of the amalgamated four-dimensional concept of time-space. Now, intervals of space are always associated with intervals of time, so that the concept of the same moment in two different places is devoid of absolute meaning. The entire history of a system, past and future, must be considered in existence only together, on one hand. On the other hand, if a body is in motion at a high speed compared with the speed of light, a clock attached to that body will slow down. We say that time undergoes a dilation.

At cosmological levels, high speeds are not a rare occurrence at all. A first observation is that we cannot consider a universal time valid in any part of the known universe. To make things clearer we have to show that today there are about 100 billion known galaxies, and each one may contain, on an average, about 100 billion stars. This was the stuff taken into account by Dr. Gerald L. Schroeder when he wrote *Genesis and the Big Bang*.[6] Some details for the general reader about this aspect were given by Dr. Schroeder in a second book, The Science of God, published in 1997 by Free Press. But in order to understand what is going on at the scale of the entire universe, we must consider Einstein's General Theory of Relativity, given by its author in 1915, where it is shown that the behavior of space and time depends on the density of matter present in the universe. For instance, when placed on the surface of a dense star, a clock will slow down; by how much will depend on the star's density.

Today there are known celestial bodies with densities between 100,000 billion to one million billion grams per cubic centimeter. If we compared the time shown by such a clock with another one located on the surface of the Earth, there would be a tremendous difference. Therefore, a universal clock

---

[6] Gerald L. Schroeder *Genesis and the Big Bang*.N.Y.: Bantam Books Oct.1990.

doesn't exist. When Einstein's equations are applied for the gravitational slowing down of time to the entire known mass of the universe, something unbelievable happens, but it can be checked, since the changes in the flow of time can be measured. We say that in a strong gravitational field, time slows down. The data used by Gerald Schroeder are: the mass of the known universe given in kilograms is 10^{53} (which means that the number one is followed by 53 zeroes). The estimated radius of the universe, made up by the specified matter was taken as ten billion light years (one light year being the distance travelled by light during one year, and the speed of light is 300,000 kilometers per second). With the above data at his disposal, Dr. Schroeder calculated the gravitational potential at the hypothetical edge of the universe and the time dilation caused. Then a clock is slowed down by a factor of approximately one million relative to a clock functioning on the less massive Earth. If we translate this result into minutes, this means that the passage of one minute marked by a clock placed at the edge of the universe will correspond to a million minutes of a clock that measures the time on the surface of the Earth. In terms of days, years, and millennia, it means that this slowing down by a factor of a million makes the giant step that explains how 15 billion cosmological years are reduced to six days of the Hebrew Bible that represent the time of creation. Thus, the Hebrew Bible and science are both correct, but such an astonishing result shows again the extra-human dimension of the statement made more than three thousand years ago regarding creation.

As we may figure out from the foregoing presentation, the billion-year measurement of the age of the universe represents a result according to clocks working at the Earth's current gravitational potential. But when Genesis says six days passed before man was created, the Hebrew Bible is speaking of a system that included all the universe. This is why the Hebrew

Bible's terminology is so different from the terminology for the ages when describing the passage of time.

It has to be noted that from the time of man's presence on the surface of the Earth, the dates of events described in the Hebrew Bible are matched by archeological findings. The post-Adam happenings are dated in the Hebrew Bible by the ages of generations of humans who populated the Earth and the flow of time that they recorded was therefore similar to our flow of time. As Dr. Schroeder specified, in these calculations he used some data that usually contain a degree of uncertainty, but the calculations are based on a physical theory that is increasingly confirmed by experiments.

We live in a world built up by different well-organized sets. Stars are grouped into galaxies, galaxies are grouped into clusters, clusters are grouped into superclusters, etc. It has been proved that the universe started a number of billion years ago. Therefore, all the atoms that make up the entire matter in the universe were packed together in the distant past before any being existed. But every stone and every being is made up of the same initial stuff containing the same kind of atoms. In this sense, we have in our mind and body something from the most distant stars which fires our mind, pushing in an active restless way the human curiosity and imagination. Our brains, matter organized on a superior level, maintain the human ability to return to the origins by discovering the laws that govern the physical world.

The human brain, by its structure, has embedded within it a tremendous amount of possibilities. That amount of matter that belongs to every human has a mass of between one and two kilograms, another great mystery of creation. In this sense, some thinkers say that God is in everyone's head, since the human brain by itself is something divine by the way it is made up. Indeed, thinking is located here, and through the process of thinking, you can "catch" the laws of nature using some mathematics, and build up via the same process. In a more abstract way, we might say that the human mind can discover some structures of the physical world. It is more than amazing: it is wonderful. It's like the self feeling a touch of the divine, without using any sensory organs.

The atheist, as well as the agnostic, has to examine the concept of Almighty held by Jewish sources. Only there, by using his mind, will he find this concept of one parameter, undistorted, without the anthropomorphic intermingling that is completely foreign to Judaism. Perhaps it will be easier for everyone to understand why those religions that became universal had to be based on the Jewish concept of God. The facts presented in the previous sections show that science picks up the essence of different phenomena from nature, and is the most important supplier for the entire body of human knowledge, giving it back: simplified, clarified, and, I would dare to say, glorified.

3.9

A Physical System and Its Evolution

The fifth proof pertains to the evolution of a physical system. The system under consideration is the entire universe. As it is specified in the Hebrew Bible, at the beginning it was chaos. We must take into account the important aspect that such a physical system is an isolated one. Therefore, no outside element can eventually intervene in any way to influence the system under consideration. There is a branch of physics called thermodynamics (mentioned earlier), and according to it, a function of state called entropy is introduced. This function measures the degree of disorder of a system. The disorder tends to increase if things are left to themselves. One can create order out of disorder, but to do that requires expenditure of work, or energy, and so the amount of energy available decreases in time.

It is a matter of common experience that the entropy of an isolated system always increases; and when two systems are joined together, the entropy of the combined system is greater than the sum of entropies of each system. What we just explained is known under the name of the Second Law of Thermodynamics. Our universe started as a very hot system; to cool it down and expand, an exterior intervention, was necessary, something that is a part of the world and at the same time out of it. The reader may call that outside thing intervention or whatever he likes, but the facts remain, and they cannot be changed, regardless of the readers' point of view.

3.10

Pure Math and the Universal Constructor

Another interesting observation, the sixth one, may be brought up here. At first look it regards pure mathematics, and the topic is known under the name cellular automata theory. It was initially introduced by two mathematicians of Jewish descent, John von Neuman and Stanislaw Ulam, for self-reproduction in biological systems being developed by other mathematicians for a wide range of applications.

We are interested in one general aspect developed by Von Neuman in his book, Theory of Self-Reproducing Automata. He proved rigorously that it is possible for a universal constructor to exist. He found that self-reproduction can occur when, and only when, the machine exceeds a certain threshold of complication. We may say that he demonstrated the interesting fact that a physical system can take on new properties, reproducing itself, when it possesses a certain complexity. Since this is a general demonstration, it can be applied to the entire universe. The big question here is how, from a total lack of complexity, matter could build up systems on different levels of complexity with a very high precision. For the "pure" unbeliever, there has to exist a "super duper computer" capable of doing the job. But where such a machine would come from is another story, one that he is unable to explain. We suppose that the result is self-explanatory and that the reader may draw his own conclusion.

3.11

Science, Social Life and the Jewish Religion

The presentation made in the last sections showed different aspects of interpretation of two domains: science and the basis of Jewish religion. Now we will present, briefly, some aspects of the ways in which they are related to one another. In order to translate such a purpose into fact, we will be forced sometimes to make parallels once again between phenomena that belong to a specialized branch of science and those of the Hebrew Bible. We would like to mention the important fact that other religious systems, based on the Hebrew Bible and its invariant elements, may derive some advantages by using our proofs, even though the author did not envision any other system of faith beyond Judaism. Our purpose is to draw, in a schematic way, the role played by the individual, the indivisible constituent element of the social body, resembling the atom, the basic brick of any substance.

One may foresee the complexity of the problems solved by the Jewish system, starting with deep antiquity, since the variables of a social state of affairs are not given just once and forever. Some social changes intervene, the most important being:

1.) The continual progress of the human element.
2.) The change in relations among the individuals (for instance, when some of them pass from one social group to another).
3.) New technological advances determine what may be called exterior actions of a social group that induce changes in the entire social body.

All three points presented here are interconnected. For instance, the third one will head to changes in the second one, and the second one will influence the first one, which undergoes changes due to the natural growth of the population. The variability of influences and relations that intervene according to the previous statements, may be grouped as follows:

a.) The morality of the individuals that comprises the norms of behavior in family and society;
b.) The legislation of a society;
c.) The economy of a society (that has to do with the production, distribution, and consumption of goods and services);
d.) The intellectual growth of a society.

Within the framework of such a multitude of facts, where each group represents an undetermined set, all interdependent in different ways, the Hebrew Bible has succeeded in building up the foundation of order and assessment that remains valid at any time, in any civilized human community. The Hebrew Bible doesn't present any kind of Rorschach pattern to interpret; it doesn't give interpretations at all. Crystal clear are all axioms, their purpose being to hasten the pace of discovery and understanding needed to develop and push forward mankind. As we already noticed, since the axioms of Judaism are irreducible and invariant in time, and were given so many years ago to mankind, they are attributed to a unique universal power that reveals itself by acting in specific ways for animates and inanimates.

What man discovered in both sectors, the Hebrew Bible and

science, are usually called laws of nature; day by day he tries to study those laws to learn how the human condition can be improved, taking into account all points specified at the beginning of the present section. In colleges and universities, students will get, during their years of study, a certain experience which has to be used later in life. At that time, they cannot get all necessary directions on how to solve any specific problem out of the academic field. Such a college or university doesn't exist. The most important thing is that the student of yesterday got a good training in the basic disciplines, which helped him later to confront successfully different problems in life.

Within the framework of different scientific disciplines were developed methods valid for a definite domain. Phenomena considered by some believers as manifestations of providence became classified within the framework of the so-called natural sciences. There appeared to be a conjunction between science and some aspects of religion, which some considered an invasion of domains. We may say that, by instinct, the human creature felt that the basic rules of the Hebrew Bible contained that "substance" which, in our day, is attributed to natural laws called unchangeable. Each individual, according to his educational background in different moments of history tried to explain, at least for himself, different phenomena. His interpretations were limited, as the possibilities of each human are, but in time, the continuous forward motion of human knowledge shows what is right and what is wrong. The juxtaposition of some random deductions, to one or another invariant element, could not enrich the human knowledge or condition. In time, the situation has been repeated, and entire generations continue the predecessors' custom of adding new observations without resorting to the axioms. Only in such cases can we discover discrepancies, and sometimes their nature was far removed from ethics.

As we mentioned earlier in this section, our intention is not to consider any other religious system; however, an example will be given. We are justified in using it by the suffering inflicted on our people during centuries of persecutions by those who tried to teach us our heritage and our duty according to that heritage. We mention them here because the mistakes of yesterday will show how to avoid any recurrence tomorrow. The Roman Catholic Church embraced Aristotle's point of view regarding the position of the Earth in our universe as being central. The Hebrew Bible with its invariant axioms says clearly the human is a central figure in the universe. This is true, indeed, since only the human element is able to enrich (or destroy) what the unique interaction created. The fact that the Roman Catholic Church attached such a point of view to the Hebrew Bible could not change anything (we are talking about that part of the Hebrew Bible used by the Roman Catholic Church). Of course, the Jews couldn't agree with such a point of view. Physics, and the other two sisters, mathematics and chemistry, swept away any inaccuracy, and the truth has been restated.

The invariants mentioned in chapter one were powerful tools in understanding how we can test the heritage left by different generations of our forbearers. There is another aspect regarding the scientific disciplines. Each branch of science uses its own methods to investigate different phenomena. In other words, we find here a specific restricted domain of activity. But those involved in research need the moral elements of the Decalogue. Just as in college they needed elements to face problems in their field, so the moral standards prescribed by the Decalogue could give them the necessary ethical background to face life in the specialized domain. If those standards are not respected, there is a danger that a terrible anarchy could prevail in any domain of research, including those sectors where we may suppose that only pure atheists work.

The Hebrew Bible tries to avoid such words as predestination, since if such a concept is applied to humans it would mean that the place of every human element in the social body would be established from the moment of birth, and no one could do anything about it. However, this point of view is completely foreign to Judaism, being against basic Jewish beliefs. Indeed, the Hebrew Bible shows many times how such changes, at all levels, may occur. From the consideration of facts, and only facts, in the environment where we live and work day by day, indications from all sides are overwhelming in giving us a powerful push toward the impression of design. Starting with unicellular organisms and ending with stars, galaxies, and other exotic objects, their life as well as their rebirth gives one a feeling that there is something that is a part of this world but again, doesn't belong to it. Of course, we base our conclusions finally only on facts and not on impressions; this is why we have already used a number of scientific proofs.

We would like to underscore that a scientist, atheist or not, may gain an inestimable treasure of knowledge for human society. His findings are situated by themselves, above politics, race, or the social layer to which he belongs. The results for research in a free, open world constitute a common value for all men, brothers as they are, according to the Hebrew Bible, as well as the scientific gathered data.

Before we close the present section, we would like to consider another aspect of social life. In any society that has reached a certain cultural level, some internal social forces eventually start to press for changes. Here lies the problem that has to be solved: How can righteousness and charity be combined? There is a balance: on one side lies what is right and on the other is, or should be, the humanitarian understanding.

The Hebrew Bible with its everlasting basic rules foretold such an evolution. It proclaimed equal rights for all mankind, realizing that balance. As we know, the Hebrews left slavery behind. They had to live under the powerful influence of that "civilized Egypt," where fighting among different gods, representatives of different domains, had been a daily event. They also had to endure the excessive work under Egyptian taskmasters in order to prepare beautiful tombs to house the pharaohs after their deaths. The duties regarding life after death were so many and so complex that no time remained to enjoy being alive.

The oriental philosophy tried to find an acceptable explanation, at least from a theoretical point of view: it considered that, on the stage of life, humans are in equal measure actors and spectators. Then there is a balance, in fact, since the solution is comprised in its organization. But how can this be, in a society whose organization is inconceivable without slavery? The Hebrew Bible swept away this kind of attitude, and according to its norms, we may consider ourselves stage managers and spectators. Indeed, the complex human creature succeeded in putting on stage all human joy and tragedy; only then did he sit down with his fellows as spectator and critic. He tried to polish each role to a high degree of perfection, according to existing conditions, and condemned slavery. As we can see, it has been possible to overcome difficulties in the social field with the appearance of the ethical rules contained in the axioms of the Hebrew Bible, and to satisfy those points enumerated at the beginning of this section. Using those rules as a guide in building up a society, a satisfactory relationship between righteousness and charity could be reached in each epoch of human society, including the contemporary one.

3.12

Negation and Reality

To underscore once more the importance of the ethics on which a society is based, we are going to consider another domain linked to the education of the members of a given society, namely, literature. We know that some writers, experiencing different negative aspects of social life, reach certain conclusions and create the so-called "literature of absurdity." They probably reached such conclusions by observing that the way in which a society is organized and acts has, as a guide, certain laws based upon logic, which try to conduct the community toward civilized living. However, the unrestricted behavior of some governments was against elementary logic, and had nothing to do with a civilized society.

For instance, Euclidean geometry (the geometry currently taught at the high-school level and currently used in everyday applications, engineering included) is based on a number of postulates. By negating the fifth postulate, a completely new geometry emerged.[7] In the same way, those writers, true researchers of the human psyche, started to negate the standard accepted ethical rules used in organizing a civilized society. By introducing modifications, they built up, in their writings, a social structure in which the entire society behaves according to the modified changes. Thus were Kafka's literary

---

[7] Through a point exterior to a line, only one parellel can be drawn to that line.

works created and presented with a strong artistic force. Unfortunately, it has been confirmed that it is possible for the human species to descend to a very low level, when such distorted social relations become a fact of daily life. The fascist society represented the most repulsive prototype and may serve the entire world as model of what it means to negate the ethical elements contained in the axioms of Judaism.

While the new geometry obtained by the negation of the fifth postulate proved to be fruitful, a society whose ethical norms become negated could endanger the entire human species. Such a miserable result of human activity shows that the complex human creature has to draw certain conclusions and set up limits in the domains linked to his practice. The seriousness of any conclusion has to contain something essential linked to invariance, its relative character resulting from its attachment to a certain domain. No axiom or conservation law regarding a human social body may use ambiguous concepts. An old folkloric Jewish song says (in its essence): "little Jew, carry on your back your little bag: the Holy Torah." He did indeed, all the time, and he continues to carry it.

But the countries of the Old Europe made every possible effort to torture this people, despite the fact that it represented an evident element of progress. Forced out of their country as believers in their abstract, unique God, persecuted without grounds by those who normally had to be their most ferocious defenders, robbed and sometimes killed by their persecutors, the Jews moved from village to village, from city to city, from country to country, lacking food and shelter, at the mercy of every outlaw. But they did not give up. Even the majority of Christian bishops, blinded by hate, did not see that they had in front of them the most sublime example of belief, the unique source that could be helpful in their work as spiritual leaders.

It is absolutely impossible to understand or explain how

the Church could not see the importance represented for all religions based on the Hebrew Bible of the existence of the Jewish people of Israel. She had at hand the chosen people, the carriers of their unique treasure, the people who gave the founder of the Church itself, who struggled, by all means, to penetrate the deep meaning of the Book of Books. A loyal cooperation could bring the Christian Church incomparably more benefits than any other means used to propagate its creed among those people who did not belong to the House of Israel. Their founder created for them a new religion, with fewer obligations (for the children of Noah), showing them the way of the unique God in a corresponding frame of reference. But the great majority of the clergy chose another way, propagating hatred, and only time has shown how wrong they were.

Such a teaching is not only without any links to the Hebrew Bible, but is directly against it. In spite of all those persecutions, impossible to describe, the Jews kept their promise and continued to provide the greatest percentage of clergymen and scientists, according to the indications of the Hebrew Bible. This was the promise that Israel made to the unique supreme power in the Sinai Desert (nobody's land, since those axioms are valid for everybody). Here, Israel received the title of the Chosen People, not as a privilege, but as having a number of supplementary obligations. We are talking here about facts recorded by history, and therefore they cannot be denied. The scattering of the Jewish people in all corners of the earth, in the Diaspora, showed how a phantom could be resuscitated, brought back to life, due to its ethical system, astonishing the entire world by the results obtained. Indeed, in every part of the world where someone tried to organize a fight for righteousness or freedom, or advance ideas regarding the human elements or the human society, one could always find in the frontline, members of the Jewish community. In other words, the Jews didn't miss any barricade. But how many times has a new government installed with active Jewish help, after an interval of time, begun to use the same retrograde way as their predecessors to poison the atmosphere with anti-Jewish propaganda.

3.13

Judaism and Method

As we could see, the Hebrew Bible uses a philosophy that is expressed in accessible language. Thus, any member of a community willing to spend the time is able to comprehend its basic rules. Thus, Judaism succeeded in realizing a unity between its theoretical foundation and the rules of daily life. The Jewish philosophy was built up in a way able to meet the social realities of life for all: farmers, craftsmen, businessmen, soldiers, statesmen, intellectuals, scientists, etc., unifying them by the simple evident fact that all belong to the human race. For the groups aforementioned, there are different points of view, as well as distinct goals, that represent important realities. In order to make oneself understood by those groups, one has to use the language specified above, as well as concepts that seem to belong to naive, but not simplistic, realism. Otherwise, the possibility of any understanding becomes a failure.

Therefore, it was necessary to find the elements that would appeal to all social layers, helping them to understand the realities of their world in a clear, explicit, and precise way. It was not the first time such an attempt was made, but the entire buildup was out of use when the conditions started to be different, and a harbinger knocked at the door requiring radical changes of that society. The basic elements used in the entire construction had to maintain their timeless freshness; we mean their functional value, regardless of the changes that occurred for the entire social body in its structure. This is why a judicial unbiased written code applicable to all mentioned social layers has been elaborated.

Of course, some other people had their codes written too. Thus, the Sumerians are known to have had a code written 2500 B.C. Five hundred years later, that code was augmented by the Babylonians into the previously mentioned code of Hammurabi. The Egyptians also had a code or law in the second century B.C. We emphasize here the important fact that none of the law codes that predated Moses included the great, democratic, and invariant spirit of the law embedded in the Torah. The functional power of all of them passed away simultaneously with their society. Moses' code eclipsed all previously known codes, not only by its passion for justice, its humanism, and its love for democracy, but mainly by its irreducible fundamental axioms which bridged centuries and millennia, anticipating the scientific modern era. Based on the axioms of Judaism and their connection with daily life, Moses created an independent judiciary. The Mosaic law established the principle that people can do anything not denied to them. We may say that even when Moses' Law makes a positive statement, it is usually an amendment to a negative commandment.

Moses' law, based on the axioms of the Hebrew Bible, established that there is a direct contact between man and the Almighty. Strict Jewish monotheism gave the Jewish idea of kingship a completely different content compared with that of the non-Jews. The other people attributed divine descent to their king. The Jews never thought of any of their kings as being a descendent of God. On the contrary, there were no special laws for the Jewish king. Having a scientific base, Jewish laws offer rational explanations. But among some Jews, under the influence of secular teachers who do not know the basic content of the Jewish laws, there is a tendency to regard many Jewish laws as rituals. The contemporary Anglo Jewish Scholar Louis Jacobs has written: "Nowhere in the whole biblical record is there the faintest suggestion that God imposes upon man arbitrary rules which must be observed purely on the grounds that God so desires." (See Louis Jacobs, Religion and Morality, edited by Gene Outka and John P. Reeder Jr. New York 1973.)

The Hebrew word for justice means justice plus law; they cannot be separated as they are in English. Justice is an ideal and law is a rule of conduct. To make justice part of our daily life, we must work out those rules and apply them to the social body. According to the Jewish judicial system, justice means that certain laws must be obeyed by every man. The way described above is that followed by strong science. If that is the case, one cannot wonder about such achievements, more than three thousand years ago, when the basic rules of the Hebrew Bible were given. The facts underline once more the profound understanding of the human element as a part of nature, deeply rooted in it. All those facts constitute more than any human being could do; this is why we may say again that only something that could see our world from outside, contemplate it, and judge it was able to elaborate those fundamental, irreducible, and invariant rules that retain their freshness unchanged.

3.14

Reality and Judaism

Through an unconscious process the faculty of reasoning builds up invariants of perceptions, and those invariants are called, in simple, usual language real things. From here it results that all images which we make up regarding the world around us are inseparably linked to the mentioned invariants. Therefore the concept of invariant constitutes a key factor for a rational understanding of our reality in any aspect of the material world.

To emphasize the role played by the invariants in a case of reality perception, we may resort to elements linked with the physiology and anatomy of the nervous system. Thus, every nervous fiber regarding motion or perception, whether it brings tactile, visual, auditory, or thermic messages, sends a set of impulses, each one by a different fiber, in a certain place of the cortex. The messages are transmitted in a specific code and they are decoded almost instantaneously by the human brain. For instance, when somebody solves a difficult algebraic problem, from the chaotic number of signals continuously received, the invariant forms are determined. In this way, we get, finally, an organized set of impressions, then all impulses received make things recognizable. This has been made possible by the mentioned invariants.

We can see that all images built up by the human mind regarding the environment are indissolubly linked with this process. What we just presented underscores the close connection between the daily occurrences and the natural sciences.

In different stages of human development, step-by-step, a division among different domains take place. To give an example, we may consider two domains, one of them being the application of the other. Thus, the machinery construction sector provides a variety of useful devices for different purposes, i.e., cars, trucks, etc. These are nothing other than applied physics, on one hand; on the other hand, in some branches of physics different elements are used which aren't clear at all to the practitioner from the kinship field. For the practitioner, the different fields such as elementary particles, the quanta, etc., are baffling concepts. The specialist finds himself in front of a contradiction between his reality and the abstract significance of some concepts such as those considered above.

Among the specialists of the mentioned domains, a monstrous gorge is created, and each one becomes more and more a stranger to the other. To help the members of a society to feel closer to one another, a generalizing philosophy is needed to express in an unsophisticated manner the fact that the new abstract domains are not in contradiction with their belief. On the contrary, every new advance has its place in that philosophy that has to become a bridge of understanding over the dividing abyss between domains and the existing reality. Judaism acted in a corresponding way, starting with the dawn of human knowledge, eliminating any mythical element. No mythical explanation could be accepted at any level: ethical, social, strong, or soft science. Judaism started from the beginning with an abstracted entity and a distinctive modesty. It does not present Israel as the center of the earth, but as the people to whom God first revealed his presence.

Once more we are going to present an example emphasized by the Hebrew learnings, one that tries to explain another facet of the name "Chosen People." It is specified clearly that God passed the offer of his learnings first to all other nations, since all of them without exception are his children. Only at the end, after all of them turned down the offer, God came with his learnings to the children of Israel, the descendants of Jacob. Indeed, if God's learnings had been offered to all other nations first, isn't it obvious that those finally chosen have no motive to boast of themselves? If we look to the simplified scheme of the lineage tree of mankind (see next chapter), it will be easily seen that the Jewish people are located in a small corner. In the Book of Books, there is a tendency to show the human race not as being static, but rather as a dynamic system in a continuous process of evolution. Probably one of the best examples is contained in the following maxim, "Man, don't be proud about yourself, since even the worm has been created before you." The basic elements of Judaism are given in a form that constitutes a common junction among the members of any society. This is another vivid explanation of how the Jew could survive in the precarious conditions of history.

Since the present text may be read by non-Jews, or Jews who do not know too much about Judaism, we do not want to leave them with a deformed image about how to acquire enough knowledge to understand the deepest aspect of the Jewish religion, whose bases are in the Hebrew Bible. To acquire that knowledge requires hard work.

Formerly, starting at the age of five, sometimes even earlier, the Jewish child had to start the traditional school where he began to learn the Hebrew alphabet, using selected texts from the Torah. The study kept the Jewish child busy the entire day: from 8 to 12 in the morning, a break for lunch, and after this back to study. At the age of seven (maximum), this child had to enter the school of the country where he lived. Then his school time was divided between these two schools; in the morning he attended one school and in the afternoon the other. The learning process continued until night was setting in. In the small cities (shtetels) of Old Europe, the children had to have lanterns with them because the way to their homes was in full darkness; and in bad weather they had to watch their steps carefully. The author of this writing is one of the eyewitnesses of such happenings; he and his family received their Jewish education under such conditions in a city of southeastern Europe.

That was the enviroment and the conditions of the Jewish child, when at the age of five, he had to come across aseptic and antiseptoc rules as a way of civilized healthy way of life. Regarding food that could be consumed according to Moses' laws, bloody meat or meat obtained from animals fedded by remains of animals, including blood processed under any form, was strictly forbidden.

After more than three thousand years, the rest of the human society discovered the deep meaning of that Mosaic rule, unfortunately via a cruel lesson for humanity: Mad Cow Disease. The laws of keeping kosher (or the so-called kashroot rules given by Moses) specify clear: It is strictly forbidden for the Jewish human element to be a scavenger under any form.

Four

Up to the age of forty,
You live from what you eat.
After the age of forty,
You live from what you don't eat

— Ancient Jewish proverb

Chapter 4

Judaism and Daily Life

4.1

Introduction

The acquisition of new scientific data obtained in a given moment represent novelties when their discovery occurred, and they may be considered as such for a shorter or longer time. For us, those facts have an illustrative role that have been used up to now by adversaries of the Jewish religion and its base, the Hebrew Bible. Those people maintain that each new discovery hits the fixed thesis of the Hebrew Bible, which cannot follow the speed of human activity concretized in the production of new human goods and a deeper knowledge of natural laws.

Our point of view is completely different; it does not confuse the mistakes made by certain individuals in the manipulation of some fundamental concepts with the concepts themselves. Using as an example a well-known axiom from elementary geometry, we may say that those commentators cannot distinguish the fraction from the integer. But as far as we know, the fraction is smaller than the integer and then a fortiori, it will contain truncated information. If we add to all that "stuff" some misconceptions, which are the usual rule, the outcome seems to be complete. Indeed analyzing the situation, in time, we may perceive the presence of extremist representatives on both sides, without knowing exactly the essence of the problems involved.

To prove it, we recall some attitudes regarding the appearance of the Einsteinian Mechanics, when a lack of understanding of that revolutionary scientific discovery made some scientists utter incredible statements, like Einstein or Newton. This is a false statement, of course, but still a mild one.

Another one having a sharp double edge, one oriented against Jews in general, the other directed against what some anti-Semitic writers called "Jewish science" is the following: "The mathematical concepts developed today by some Jews from Poland, Russia or Germany trying to present themselves as inspired prophets make the crowd remain fascinated as though in front of a magic lantern. Those concepts appear in a form of incoherence specially made-up, showing that the genius is a form of neurosis adjacent to madness." (Louis de Launay, member of the French Academy of Sciences, The Church and Science, page 202.)

Such absurd statements did not change anything. Einstein's Theory has been confirmed by practice, and all kinds of forecasts linked with the failure of the theory have evaporated, with all goodwill of some who still try from time to time to discredit it. To reach such an understanding, a deep knowledge of physics was necessary, and only a special group of scientists, the elite of that time, could appreciate the true revolutionary ideas introduced in strong science. They could not understand that Newton has his well-deserved place at one scientific level, and Einstein at another. Where the Newtonian Mechanics stops with its possibilities, Einstein's Theory steps in.

4.2

Judaism and Universal Brotherhood

As the history of science shows, scientific results are given to the entire human community, irrespective of denigrators. If we try to go back in time and take a look at what the Hebrews did in antiquity when they made up their closed circle, trying continuously to solve problems linked to the individual life, did they not inscribe themselves heart and soul on the trajectory of research for all mankind? To make things clearer for the reader, we have made up a simplified lineage tree of mankind according to the Hebrew Bible, the first humans being Adam and Eve. After the flood, only Noah and his family remained alive. He had three sons, Sem, Ham, and Japhet. The Terrah family that lived in Babylon is the offspring of Sem. This family had three sons, Haram, Abram, and Nahor (see Fig. 2).

After Abram arrived at the concept described as ethical monotheism he, together with his wife Sarah and all his household, started their journey toward Canaan. It is important to emphasize the fact that monotheistic beliefs and/or such tendencies existed before Abram. But all of them had little in common with Abram's point of view. All those deities were subservient to nature and were restricted to a certain locality or country, the Sumerian High-God,

Anu or the Babylonian God, Shamash. Abram's God is the center of heaven, earth, and all that exists. He is independent of nature and oblivious of geographical limitations. Abram's God has a main concern, justice and righteousness. He is, therefore, first of all an ethical God.

After God revealed himself under the tetragrammaton YHWH (translated "by the Lord") and promised Abram the land as an inheritance (Genesis 15:7), the promise was ratified by a divine covenant with Abram by virtue of which he will become the founder of a new nation chosen by God for universal service, not for domination. The twofold significance of the covenant, national and universal, was accompanied by the act of circumcision, a national mark of consecration to God. At the circumcision, the patriarch's name was changed from Abram to Abraham, which means "the father of a multitude of nations, embracing all the families of the earth, who were to be blessed in him and in his offspring."[1]

Abraham's work was carried on by Isaac and continued by Jacob, one of Isaac's two sons (Jacob and Esau). God renewed the covenant with both Isaac and Jacob, with all the promises it entailed. Jacob, the grandson of Abraham, had an experience during his sleep of wrestling with a nonhuman and was named by that being, Israel, which means the human who was able to fight the super human power, or the champion of God. The name Israel replaced the name Hebrew by which the descendants of the Abrahamic family were known, because they came from the other side of the Euphrates. This term, Hebrew, is derived from a root meaning the other side. That fight is another way of the Creator, emphasizing how His

---

[1] Before Sarah became pregnant with Isaac, desperate by not having a child, she asked Abram to have a child with their maid, the Egyptian, Hagar. After a while, Hagar gave birth to a son called Ishmael. According to the Hebrew Bible, the Arabs are the descendants of Ishmael.

human creature can acquire the needed knowledge to conquer the natural laws in order to improve its human condition.

There is another dream linked with our forefather Jacob (Genesis 28). In that dream, Jacob saw a ladder supported at one end by the Earth and extending into the heavens. This dream was clearly meant to show that the human element, as a creation of the Supreme Ruler, can reach any place in the universe; nothing is forbidden him, with one exception: He will never learn who is supporting the other end of the ladder. In order to attain it, he needs endless knowledge.

Jacob had twelve sons who became the progenitors of the Twelve Tribes, constituting the people of Israel (see section 3.5). He and his family went into Egypt from Canaan; a terrible drought had driven them out looking for food. One of his sons, Joseph, through a combination of events, rose from a very lowly position to that of viceroy of Egypt (Genesis 37-50). In time, the status of the children of Israel changed. From free men, they were turned into slaves. In a critical moment of their history, there arose a national liberator with a universal vision — Moses. All nations of Africa came out from the offsprings of Ham, and from those of Japhet the northern nations (see Fig. 2).

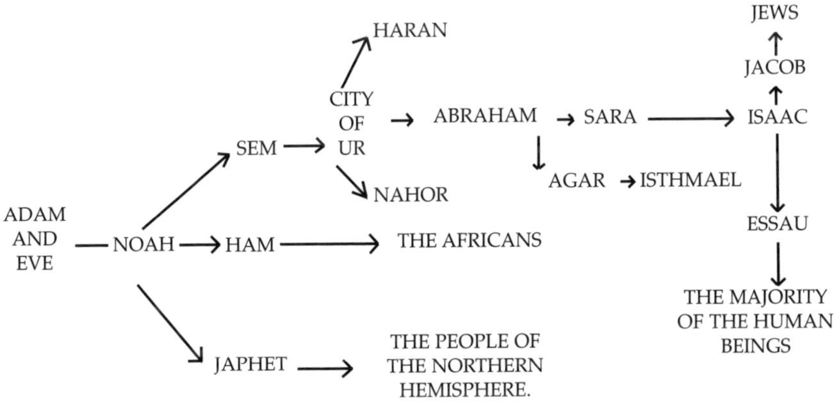

Fig. 2. Simplified Chart of the Genealogical Lineage of Human Race

All humans on earth are their descendants, and their evolution occurred in different places and, of course, in different conditions. The moral drawn from the simplified chart is obvious: Can someone admit, in any form, an antagonist behavior among brothers? Here a question isn't out of place. If a people reached such a high degree of understanding, should they use such an example? The answer is yes. Any axiom, it doesn't matter in what way it is stated, has to be used after this to build up some theories and/or legislations which have to be less abstract, flexible, able to answer to some practical problems occurring in everyday life. Then using elements of understanding at every level, in any epoch, those elements could reach the entire human species because all of them have common descendants and equal rights in any part of their common home, our terra. From the previously mentioned simplified chart, it is more than clear that Judaism is the unquestionable source of an ideal, universal brotherhood.

4.3

Abstract Thinking and the Epoch

Any novelty we want to introduce, in a field of human activity, has to be at the level of understanding of the contemporaries. If your fellow men do not understand your new thought, it is as though you are talking to them in a foreign language. Abstract thinking started to be more common in contemporary science: physics and its good sister, mathematics. It is one of the reasons why our forefathers were not understood in antiquity by other nations. We hope an example will serve to make things clearer.

Looking retrospectively, we will mention an event that occurred approximately two thousand years ago. The Romans, one of the most civilized people of that time, couldn't understand the Jewish abstract thinking. They believed that in the place of the Jewish Temple, called the Holy of Holiest, there must be something material that can be touched. Otherwise, what is the reason behind all religious ceremonies when, once a year, only the great Jewish priest may open it? The unique invisible God was for them nothing more than a crazy idea of Jewish stubbornness.

When the Roman soldiers penetrated the walls of the Jewish fortress of Jerusalem after heavy fighting, their official military commander, Titus Flavius Vespasian, was impatient to see what was hidden in that sacred place. In a rush he opened it and, blinded by his victory, the Roman general saw nothing. Then he started to say: "Crazy, absolutely crazy people."

Paying more attention to the contents, he found scrolls written in an unknown language.

Furious at not finding something tangibly precious in his eyes, he opened the first scroll, where square Hebrew letters written in a perfect order, like soldiers of a disciplined army, faced him; but instead of weapons pointed against his army, he saw a depicted smile. The rows of those letters gave him the feeling that the depicted smile was increasing in intensity, transforming itself in a powerful laughter. Fascinated, he continued to look at them, and became furious. According to eyewitnesses, he took out his sword and cut the first scroll. Looking at it, his anger increased. He started to see in all those well-aligned letter fighters something incomparably more powerful than his entire well-disciplined army. Indeed, from all those scrolls, like a unique stream, came out from the Jewish fighters' mouths reaching his ears: "Listen Israel, Your God is Unique, He is only One." Titus, his armies, and all their splendor vanished, but the Hebrew square letters are alive and continue to propagate the same eternal rules adopted in our day by any civilized nation. Christianity made its appearance on Jewish soil and soul inside the "Promised Land" as a sect of the Jewish religion. The first Christians were Jews, and they didn't consider themselves otherwise. Their first spiritual leaders tried to modify what we may call the potential functions of Judaism. For instance, the Christian leaders replaced the Lex talionis by the aphorism, when someone slaps you on one cheek, offer him the other as well. Their desire was to show

---

2 Christianity has its foundation the Hebrew Bible; recognizes that Adam and Eve were the parents of mankind, from where it is easy to recognize an existent brotherhood among all human beings. Trying to convince the Jews about some prophecies, in certain places of the Hebrew Bible, misleading translations were intentionally made since Paul of Tarsus was chiefly concerned with building up a powerful church capable or attracting new converts. In our days serious Christian scholars could identify those intercalations that constitute a change in the Hebrew text.

that the slap was given to a brother and, if he made a mistake, forgive him.[2] From the Jewish territory, the Christian faith spread out over the entire Old Europe. It is interesting to notice the fact that the European Christianity has little to do with the initial one.

The theoretical basis of the European Christian doctrine was made up by Paul of Tarsus, who made fundamental changes in the Christian teachings. For example, after the death of the Jesus Christ, who established Christianity, his disciples continued to heed the teacher's message to observe the Jewish law (Halakha). Indeed, Acts 2:46 and 3:1 state that the disciples regularly prayed at the Temple, and Acts 10:14 records Peter's scrupulous observance of the Jewish dietary law (Kashrut). In the same line of facts may be inscribed Acts 15:1, which states "some men came down from Judea" to teach that "unless you have yourselves been circumcised in the Tradition of Moses, you cannot be saved" (those men, in line with Galatians 2:12, appear to have been sent by James, Jesus' brother). In Acts 21:14, James says to Paul, "Let everyone know there is no truth in the reports they have heard about you, and that you still regularly observe the law."

Paul of Tarsus made the great move, changing the ideology; he made a sharp difference between Judaism and Christianity, sometimes even using mistranslations of the Hebrew text. First, in Judaism God considers people's actions to be more important than their faith. Indeed it doesn't matter which Jewish congregation you will attend, no rabbi would deliver a sermon on salvation through faith which is a most common subject of the Christian sermons. The Jew has a central obligation: to act in accordance with the Hebrew Bible's law, as well as those laws derived by our sages according to the axioms of Judaism.

In the Gospel, it can be found noted that Jesus Christ and

his early followers were devoted Jews. "Do not imagine that I have come to abolish the Law or the Prophets; I have not come to abolish them, but to fulfill them," Jesus declared to his disciples. He concluded the message against the violators of Jewish law: "Therefore, the man who infringes even the least of these commandments and teaches others to do the same will be considered the least in the kingdom of heaven" (Matthew 5:17-19). Paul of Tarsus introduced in his ideology what cannot be found anywhere in the Hebrew Bible. According to his ideology, a person is cursed by God for breaking any law (Galatians 3:10-13). In Deuteronomy (27:15-25) are listed eleven basic ethical prohibitions: against violence, bribery, idolatry, incest, oppression, etc., and it declares the transgressor of any of them cursed by Jews and Moses, not by God. The Hebrew Bible uses frequently the words "Torah" and "this Torah" in reference to a specific group of laws and in the above quoted prohibitions, the Hebrew Bible refers to "this Torah." The above specified change was introduced in the Gospel.

In the Hebrew Bible, eternal damnation doesn't appear, and it is completely unknown to Judaism, as well as the word "hell." It is known that the word sheol, which means grave in Hebrew, has been translated into hell. Indeed in Genesis 37:35 our patriarch Jacob speaks of going to sheol (his grave), without seeing his son Joseph. It is obvious he doesn't speak about going to hell because the concept of hell is foreign to Judaism. Sinners who suffer eternally cannot be found anywhere in the Hebrew Bible. These concepts were introduced in the Western world through the Pauline ideology embedded in the Gospels.

The Hebrew Bible understands that people will occasionally sin. Many centuries before Paul of Tarsus, Jews were taught that God knows that there is no man who only does good. For example, the Hebrew Bible tells of Jews who sinned but, returning to the law which they violated, were restored to

God's grace. Among those who sinned for instance are listed Moses and King David. None of them was eternally cursed. Paul of Tarsus made a caricature of the law, because if God would curse men whom he created imperfect, God appears cruel and sadistic, notions completely unknown to Judaism. From Pauline doctrine has been born the major source of a pernicious myth that tries to present the Jewish God of the Hebrew Bible as a vengeful one in comparison with the Christian God of the Gospels as a loving one. But it is the same Creator of our world, our universe, and nobody is telling us anything in the Gospels about any discussion, peaceful or not, between Father and Son regarding such major changes.

According to Judaism, the good people of all nations attain salvation (Tosefta Sanhedrin 13:12), but according to Christianity the belief in Christ is the sole means of salvation (Galatians 2:21). The Son of Man has the authority to forgive sins (Matthew 9:6) but Jesus forgives all sins. That constitutes a radical departure from Judaism, since in Judaism God himself doesn't forgive all sins. He can forgive only the sins committed against Him and no more. On the Day of Atonement, the Jews pray to forgive their sins against God, as well as the sins committed by all humans regardless of their creed. A Jew has special obligations; for him, there are 613 things he has to guard. For a non-Jew, the seven laws of the children of Noah have to be respected. They are:

i.) The prohibition of idolatry.
ii.) The prohibition of blasphemy.
iii.) The prohibition of murder.
iv.) The prohibition of sexual sins.
v.) The prohibition of theft.
vi.) The prohibition of eating a limb torn from a living animal.
vii.) To set up a legal system, in order to ensure obedience to the previous six laws.

We may say that there are six negations and one yes.

The Jewish religion and philosophy didn't bother the Romans too much because it didn't go beyond the chosen people. The Jews were forbidden to recruit new converts to their religion. But their revolt against Rome was very powerful, and continued; this is why Rome finally forced them out of their country after their last revolt in the year 70. The hope of Rome was to mix the Jews with other populations belonging to the empire so that they would simply vanish.

We know the result. Our forefathers took the books they had, first of all the Torah (many times their only possession) together with their skills, and became a wandering nation among nations. The Romans vanished, and we, the offspring of the wandering nation, are able to witness to that fact, as well as to another one: the rebirth of the ancient Jewish country, robbed and destroyed by all kinds of thiefs and adventurers. Some of them end up having the guts to claim the right of ownership after destroying and stultifying Jewish holy places.

Since the first Christians were also Jews, they got from Rome the same status: driven out and scattered in the entire Roman Empire. Here took place the separation between the Christian Jewish sect and the rest of the Jewish community. As we mentioned earlier, Paul of Tarsus realized that Europe was not mature enough to understand the essence of a new religion based on the Jewish conception of God. The broad masses of the people belonging to the Roman Empire were eager for freedom. Then he tried to create a religious doctrine based on the Hebrew Bible, able to penetrate easily all European social layers. Such a doctrine could play in Europe a double role:

i.) To create the foundation of a new religion, and

ii.) To destroy the repugnant slavery system dominant in the empire.

Confronted with the unreadiness of the Europeans to

understand the invisible unique parameter on which the entire universe depends, he introduced first the changes already mentioned. Paul was Jewish, knew the Hebrew language, and it was easy for him to invert some original writings. But those changes were still not enough. His other great compromise basically comprised the following three elements:

• *Jesus, born of a woman, isn't a Jewish scholar who develops Judaism in a way to make it accessible to the entire mankind, but he is the son of the Jewish abstract God, difficult to understand. He is a man like you. He was brought nearby you by his father, that unique God of the Hebrew Bible. Believe in him, and he will bring you freedom; you will be saved.*

• *The icons had been introduced; a concrete touchable element, close to European thinking.*

• *Another palpable element introduced was the cross. The adoption of the cross is due to a Jewish custom transposed into the frame of primitive Christianity.*

For instance, any kind of symbols, items, etc., used by Jewish enemies in order to ridicule them, the Jews transformed those items, or symbols, to be used together with their holiday clothing. The custom is maintained even in our days in all Jewish orthodox communities.

It is well known that the cross was used by the Romans to kill Jesus. The Romans made fun of Him, putting on his head a crown of thorns and calling Him Jewish king. Using the mentioned Jewish custom, the cross was transformed into a basic element in the way to practice the new religion. It was a new concrete element at the level of European understanding. To crucify somebody was a common Roman punishment. For example, during the great Jewish revolt against Rome, in Jerusalem alone, 16,000 Jews were crucified.

The Roman persecutions directed against the Jews,

because of their continuous rebellion against Rome, accentuated the process that would lead definitely to a schism between Judaism and Christianity. After an interval of about 100 to 150 years, the Christians completely separated from Judaism and asked that the persecution directed against them cease. The first rulers of the Christian faith knew very well that no Jew would admit any modification of the Jewish laws based on the Torah. In front of Paul of Tarsus was the lure to gain all of Europe, and his ambition to succeed made him not only ready to compromise, but even to became anti-Jewish, since the Jews refused to follow him.

Starting to use those three mentioned elements, the way was opened for other communities to add other concrete elements and sometimes even to change the ritual. The changes introduced had three consequences:

i.) To break off relations with Judaism.

ii.) To ensure victory for the new religion.

iii.) To bring an essential contribution in the destruction of the Roman slavery state.

4.4

Human Beings and Their Limitations

We are going to present some facts linked to the belief in a unique universal God, and to underscore some aspects. One regards the Church in general and the Roman Catholic Church in particular. The main concern of this respected institution was, and still remains, in what way the Holy Scripture is handled. For the Christians, the Holy Scripture is made up of two parts: the Hebrew Bible (in which some changes were introduced, see also appendix 1) and the Gospels (called by Christians the New Testament). As mentioned in the previous section, any man has the possibility of making mistakes. Therefore, the Church being represented by human beings cannot be infallible. The Church could still avoid such errors which didn't belong to it as an institution, but they cannot be separated from the prelates at its helm. It was enough for them to apply the profound humanism, based on Jewish ethics, propagated by Jesus Christ. Being an inseparable part of that set of human beings that has had to pass through those unfriendly measures, we allow ourselves to mention three elementary mistakes made by the Church along our wandering from hamlet to hamlet, from city to city, from country to country, and from continent to continent, in order to find a quiet place in which to work and live according to the secular local laws and regulations. The Church tried:

1.) To impose its uniqueness, and to neglect the uniqueness of God.

2.) To ban scientific discoveries.
3.) To make Jewish converts, not even trying to understand the great sin committed in carrying out such acts (see also next section).

The Church forgot its mission, which she could pursue according to the Hebrew Bible: that all mankind has to respect the seven principles of Noah's children. Using that moral teaching among different nations, the Church could fulfill its mission: to teach what is right and what is wrong. If you believe in the unique God of Abraham, Isaac, Jacob, and Moses, no being can modify the mission of the Chosen People. The fight against that people is a fight against God's will. It doesn't matter what you invent linked to the Creator (supposing it is real or imagined), no one, absolutely no one, can move, even by a micron, God's will. (For the unbeliever, no natural law can be changed).

God as the king of the universe is a man-made image brought into the Jewish poetical religious writings by the Jews of antiquity. For them, the element put on the highest scale of human organization, respected by all social layers, was the king. From here, a normal conclusion results: God being unique, He is the king of the universe.

The Jewish religion is not influenced by fashion. Its invariant basis remains unchanged, as we have specified many times. We do not try to change the image presented by our forefathers regarding the unique parameter on whom the universe depends. What purpose would it serve if the old image were exchanged, let's say, for that of "president of the entire universe?"

We used the name of unique parameter to underline again the scientific aspect of the content of the Hebrew Bible (since the name given in the Book of Books and that given in pure science fulfill the same function). What may appear erroneous doesn't belong to the images of our forefathers, but rather to arbitrary interpretations which contradict the basis of the Jewish religion itself. We would like to make clear to everyone that we have no role of missionaries whatsoever, and we don't even try to compare different creeds with ours. If we mention Christianity or Islam, this will be only in the way it is linked with or tangent to the Hebrew Bible and / or Jewish persecution.

The ethics of Orthodox and Catholic Christianity are a direct product of Jewish learning. Potential functions of Judaic ethics were explicated in Christianity. Islam is only tangential to Judaism, since Islam didn't adopt the axioms of Judaism, even under the simplified form of seven obligations of Noah's children which are also invariant elements. They are monotheists but here is a problem in which we are not interested. For example, we may find statements like, God is not God, but Allah is the only one. If the name Allah is a translation into their language of the name of God, there are no contradictions; but the negation introduced seems to give a different meaning to the word.

What the Arabs like from the Hebrew Bible is that part of Fig. 2 which indicates the origin of the Arabs, and after this, declaring Abraham as being Arab and not Jewish (1,500 years before Muhammad made his appearance in history). Then the claim to territorial gains is no problem, at least for some wanderers of the Arab world who are looking for trouble not only in the Middle East but throughout the entire world. Of course, the founder of their religion tried to convince the Jews and the Christians that the only true religion was Islam. When they couldn't do it in a peaceful way, the sword was used.

Eight hundred Jews of Quraiza were beheaded; only one Jew saved his life by abjuring his religion. The women and children were sold as slaves in 627. In 629, the Jews of Khaibar were put to the sword for the same reason. Letters and messengers were sent by the founder of Islam to the kings of

Persia, Yemen, and Ethiopia, and to Emperor Heraclius, to accept his new religion. All these facts are described in the Islamic holy book, the Koran, see for example N.J. Dawod Penguing classics 1974, (pages 13-14).

The followers of Muhammad committed the greatest profanation in the history of mankind when, armed to the teeth, they came into the Jewish Promised Land and built a mosque exactly on the place where the ancient Jewish altar for the unique invisible God existed. It is, in fact, a double profanation for Jews and Christians, since Jesus Christ and his followers studied with the wise men of Israel inside that Temple. The enterprise was, and still is, a clear one: if you want to use those places holy for you, Jew or Christian, it is possible but only via Islam. We would dare to say even more: It is an insult for the entire civilized world. To show this, we have to present another aspect of the Hebrew Bible's ethics.

Abraham (see Fig. 2) had been asked by the Almighty to sacrifice his only son, Isaac, in that place where, according to tradition, was later placed the altar when the Temple of the unique God was built. At that time, many nations brought human sacrifices to their gods. According to the Hebrew Bible, the unique God, the maker of the entire universe, had finally forbidden Abraham to make such a sacrifice, replacing the child with a ram. Abraham, the first monotheist who believed in the unique universal God, tried to show to the entire world, approximately 4,500 years ago (according to geological discoveries), that the Supreme Power of this world is against such sacrifices. We add this fact to those presented earlier in order to show why this position of Islam constitutes a sacrilege and an affront to the entire civilized world.

4.5

Antique Jewish Thought and the Hebrew Bible

Rabbi Abbahu lived on the Jewish territory approximately 1900 years ago. Using the Torah and oral Jewish tradition, he wrote in the style of its epoch. While Moses taught the Jews the Torah near Mount Sinai, in the school of angels Zagzabel taught the angels, and in Gan Eden the Holy, blessed be his name, taught the right men, who are classified above the angels. One of them asked "King of the Universe, you wrote in the Torah: 'at the beginning God created the Universe and the Earth.' At the moment you created the world, there was a being? Then God answered: 'Before this world I made other worlds and because I didn't like them, they were crushed.' We may ask what remains from the statements made by some intellectuals according to whom only the fixed theories are according to the Hebrew Bible?

The next example may be more important than the previous one, since it emphasizes the role which the human element has to play in this world, according to the Torah. It goes as follows: "And Isaac asked the Almighty, 'King of the Universe, when you made the light you said in your Torah the light is good; when you made the firmament and the Earth you said that they are good. But when you made the human being you didn't say in your Torah that man is good: why Almighty?" Then God answered. 'I didn't mention this, since the human being isn't perfect; through Torah he has to improve himself and to make better the world where he lives."

The last story we will consider in this section involves Isaiah, one of the prophets of Israel (approximately contemporary with Aristotle). According to the same style, the prophet had a discussion with an angel who took Isaiah with him, ascending for a while above the Earth. At the end of their trip, the angel asked the prophet if he liked the trip. Isaiah said: "I liked it, but it was for a short time; I spent only two hours above." Then the angel answered: "You are making a big mistake; while we spent two hours above, on the earth, 32 years passed!"

A modern man, even a scientist who lived, let say's in 1900, armed with the science of Newtonian Mechanics, a convinced atheist based on the last achievements of the human mind, would be in a hurry to utter: Give me the initial data and I will forecast for you the evolution of any physical system. The statements made by Isaiah, according to Jewish writings, are confusing and even strange. First, how could an angel fly with him? Second, how could thirty-two years pass on the surface of the earth while in the frame of reference, Isaiah spent only two hours?

The all-conquering Newtonian Mechanics shows us, in a very precise way, that time is independent of the frame of reference used. But we now know the story has a perfect meaning! The statements regarding time aren't erroneous at all. The Einsteinian Mechanics shows very clearly that this may occur. If the previously mentioned atheist passed away before 1905, he carried to his grave the firm belief that the story just related is one of the usual mystifications found in the field of religion. That knowledgeable individual was, at that time, in the possession of a mechanics that was valid for velocities which are small in comparison with the speed of light. The results are in excellent agreement with reality for high speeds. The lack of necessary scientific knowledge made him sure about his statements.

We confess that we don't know how the rendezvous between Isaiah and the angel took place. Perhaps our imagination doesn't help enough to place us within the frame of reference of ancient descriptions. In antiquity, all kinds of real problems were presented in an allegorical way, in the form of a story. Going back to the last problem, we have to underline again the fact there is a precise physical significance regarding the relativistic aspect of time running differently in different frames of reference. The last problem connected with Isaiah, with small modifications, is known in the scientific world as the twins problem. It was elaborated on the basis of Einstein's Special Theory of Relativity published in 1905, and its solution was given after Einstein published his General Theory of Relativity in 1915.

The last example shows, perhaps in a more pregnant way, how a comparison of data gathered and handled by pure science with some writings based on a careful study of the Hebrew Bible, must be done prudently. The limitation of knowledge of an individual in a certain moment of history may anathematize a passage from pure ignorance without any special intention.

Therefore, starting with two thousand years ago, the Torah has taught the Jews that creation itself is unfinished. Something of the primeval chaos was left, and mankind had been charged with the task of making order and to finish creation itself. The guidelines for that huge task are in the Torah, where everlasting prescriptions can be found by those who learn to read it and penetrate its wisdom. As we all know, that content was given to Moses and his people as custodians of that wisdom which is preserved for the entire mankind. This is why the religious Jew never needed to worship something tangible; he couldn't be influenced by other beliefs, since he considered that the Torah signified two important things:

1.) God's presence in the world.

2.) The deepest link between God and one of his creations that has to finish his work.

We dare say that Judaism is a blueprint of action inside the philosophy and ideology elaborated via the invariant elements of the Jewish faith given on Sinai. This is why Judaism acted on the tolerant principle: rather blur the differences than burn the dissidents that are God's creatures.

This point of view gave Judaism the necessary flexibility to adapt to different conditions, and to pass successfully through history. Its power can be explained in our days, with the help of pure science. The Jewish religion, having a scientific foundation, has its own distinctive view of many different issues. It is coherent and yet pluralistic, oriented in action, traditional and fully responsive to present needs. God spoke for the first time not in German, French, English, Russian, or Arabic, but in Hebrew, the language of a small people who knew how to defend their learnings through history, despite incredible adversities.

4.6

Judaism and Practice

According to historical facts, for example the Babylonian, Assyrian, Chaldeian, Egyptian, Greek, Roman, and other known civilizations passed through the following phases:

i.) Birth
ii.) Growth
iii.) Blossoming
iv.) Decrease
v.) Death

There is only one ancient exception: the Jewish one. First, how could such an exception occur? Second, given the harsh conditions in which the Jews were forced to live, how could they survive and bring about significant contributions to important domains of the civilized world? In the following, we will try to get some additional hints, besides those considered already, that may help to find a reasonable answer.

The religions of civilized countries of antiquity were busy with the interpretations of phenomena, trying to use their imagination, which was completely out of touch with natural and social phenomena. What was important had been postponed for the realm of shadows when the human element had to follow a certain way, in conformity with one or another interpretation. The religious-philosophical system that started having as its aim the direction, administration, organization, and conduct social affairs for the welfare of the entire human community as we could see was the Judaic one. Based on it were elaborate judicial laws regarding the state. In the center of its attention was located the most important element of our society: the human being.

His school and general education had to be organized for each community, small or large, and free of charge. To be paid for teaching your fellow man was considered a sin. The concern for health, food, children and their well-being, as well as the progress of the entire society, constituted the main target. Even during the conditions of Diaspora, the system of education was organized in such a way that no illiteracy could exist. It is a well-known fact that the only people practically without illiterates through history are the Jews. Every member of a Jewish community regardless of its location, had to be able to read his or her daily prayer book. Together with reading, writing was studied too. The situation has been maintained even when the living conditions for them were the worst possible. "No illiterate child" was for the Jews not a slogan but an injunction. If somebody lacked the necessary means to send his/her child to the traditional school, by a compulsory regulation of the local Jewish community, the child was taken to school and taught from a special community budget created for such purposes, its name being Talmud Torah.

But still, the hindrances were endless; for instance the slogans of sad memory like numerus clausus (which asked for a limited number of Jewish children in school) and numerus nullius (which asked for a zero number of Jewish children in school) were applied without distinction, for rich and poor of Jewish descent. If some local authorities considered it insufficient discrimination, the Old European system allowed them to do even more. But the Jews did not surrender. Judaism, starting with its dawn, has insisted that the business of religion is to teach men, to enrich their basic knowledge; only then will they be able to act more justly and more kindly toward one another.

This interpenetration of Jewish learning has developed a system of good deeds which has extended far beyond the chosen people, since all men are brothers (see Fig. 2). So Judaism addresses:

- the individual
- the individual's community
- the Jewish people, and urges that certain ideals be embodied in their daily life.

All these things could be carried out only by continuously acquiring new knowledge, enriching the general background, and preparing each member to be useful to the society where he lives. Thus law and jurisprudence, ethics and morality, as well as medicine, hygiene, astronomy, economics, and government, were included in the Talmud, which is based on the Torah (see appendix D). Therefore, the Talmud opened new vistas for the Jews, expanding their intellectual horizon, not by discarding the old, but by showing how the basic old remains unchanged and helps to penetrate into the new, applying it to daily life, and injecting new visions into social development. Therefore, the study of their religion opened for the Jews the way to become lawyers, physicians, philosophers, mathematicians, astronomers, poets, businessmen, and physicists.

Studying the Torah and the additional writings based on it, such as the Talmud (Mishna and Gemara), the Jew received a universal education. After a period of ten to fifteen years, studying the previously mentioned books, it is no wonder that the Jews had an affinity for intellectual achievements. The Talmud of abstractions and logic had sharpened their minds and opened for them new horizons for modern times. So the Jews were always, and still are, active agents in different fields, not passive bystanders. Here we can find an explanation for the fact that the persecuted Jew, usually poor, embittered, living in a hostile world, could realize sublime achievements. Daily successes in the domain of intellectual exercise, generation after generation, during decades, centuries, millennia, when his only friends were his books, made him believe what the Hebrew Bible says: When you are sowing continuously in the field of culture, you are going to gather your crops in shouts of joy. What could be taken away from the Jew in the Diaspora was, first, his money. After this, all his belongings, and not very rarely, even his life. But never his knowledge and skills.

We must remember here those instances when the Jewish holy books, together with secular books, were burned in public places. Jewish history recorded with fidelity such barbarian events which show the inhospitality of the European ground. However, many times Jewish medical doctors were called to heal those who had ordered anti-Jewish measures. Those qualified professionals of high morality understood the call of a human being in need, forgetting for the time who created the situation when he and his fellow Jews had to hide in order to save their lives. Such sublime attitudes, to save a human life from the jaws of death, sometimes brought a diminishing of the anti-Jewish attitudes.

During the medieval period, (when the Crusades were in full swing), such examples were not rare. High qualifications gave the hunted Jew a supplementary degree of freedom, which allowed him, from time to time, to jump from his humble position to help his fellow man belonging to a different layer of human society. Of course, the gain of knowledge meant work and continued effort, and for a Jew, any effort was multiplied by a lot of hindrances. But this didn't stop him or even slow him down. He started each time full of hope to achieve new cognizance, a stimulant for the psyche and intellect.

In the opinion of some psychiatrists, it seems that to go back to a physiological zero before making a new start constitutes a well of health. This point of view belongs to Judaism, which used this procedure along its millenary existence, and it is good for its denigrators to hear it again. Instead of throwing dirt at the high-priced diamonds crystallized into the basic axioms of Judaic ethics, it would be useful for them to try to get new knowledge by studying the sources. Then, knowing the truth, they would be able to make a qualified choice in order to decide what has to be thrown away: the anti-semitic hatred or the culture?

4.7

Some Data Regarding the Jewish Oppression

We are going to consider this subject in a very restrictive way, since in a digest like this, one cannot discuss the monstrous situations through which our ancestors had to pass during their millenary forced journey, practically to every corner of the terra. Entire volumes are needed to describe them, but we are not sure that the intensity of those events can be supported by the paper on which they are eventually recorded. A pale image of some events that we consider from a historical point of view as being high boiling points will be given in the table that follows; the years mentioned are given according to the contemporary era.

115	The Jews were expelled from Cyprus.
626	The Jewish tribe of Al-Nadhir, was crushed and expelled.
627	The Jewish tribe of Quraiza raided by Mohammed: some 800 men beheaded (only one Jew abjuring his religion saved his life). All children and women were sold as slaves.
629	The Jews of Khaibar were put to the sword.
640, 721, 787	The Jews of the Byzantine Empire were christianized by force.

1096	The Crusaders massacred the Jews of the European cities and towns through which they passed on their way to liberate Jerusalem from the Muslims.
1099	The Jewish community of Jerusalem was massacred by the Crusaders.
1290	The Jews were expelled from England.
1306	The Jews were expelled from France.
1355	In the city of Toledo, Spain, 12,000 Jews were massacred.
1349-50	The Jews were expelled from Hungary.
1420	In the city of Toulouse, France, the Jewish population was massacred.
1421	The Jews were expelled from Austria.
1146, 1391	The Jews of Spain were christianized by force.
1411	
1492	Approximately 250,000 Jews were expelled from Spain; 80,000 who couldn't endure the exile converted to the Christian faith.
1495	The Jews were expelled from Lithuania.
1497	The Jews were expelled from Sardinia and Sicily.

1502	All Jews of Rhodes were converted by force, expelled, or enslaved.
1541	The Jews were expelled from the kingdom of Naples.
1648-56	More than 100,000 Jews in Poland were massacred by the Ukrainian gangs of Bogdan Hmelnitzky.
1727-1747	The Jews were expelled from different parts of Russia.
1838	Entire Jewish communities from Persia were converted to Islam by force.
1882-90	In the czarist Russia, 750,000 Jews were put into ghettos.
1891	The Jews of Moscow and Petersburg were expelled.
1871-1921	Anti-Jewish pogroms occurred in Russia.
1939–1945	The German Nazis, together with other European collaborators and the active role of the Great Mufti of Jerusalem, Haj Amin, Hitler's ally, massacred over 6,000,000 Jews.

For the first time in the history of mankind, Jews were killed in cold blood and transformed into industrial goods: soap, lampshades, gloves, etc. The soap was distributed and used by the German army and population and its origin was easy recognizable, since each piece of soap had printed on it three letters: R.J.F., (which translated from German means pure Jewish fat).

The author of the present text is an eyewitness of the existence of this kind of soap, lost by the Germans during their quick retreat when beaten by the Russian army during World War II. We participated at the funeral organized for a certain amount of such soap, whose burial took place in the Jewish cemetery of our city where the last honor was given to those many unknown men, women, and children, reciting the prayers for a dead person. So used Hitler's Germany its science and technology, to show the entire world that on their forehead is written forever the words, "Shame to The Human Race" many European nations that witnessed such a modern atrocity didn't lift ever a finger to stop it. We have to mention here that some Christians saved Jews with the risk of their life. But, it was done by a handful of people only.

1948-present	In different Arab countries (except Morocco), the present Jewish communities are persecuted, robbed, killed. Massive expulsions took place. Approximately one million Jews were robbed of their belongings and expelled.
1917	In Russia, the Jews had no rights regarding their national identity. Their millenary language (Hebrew) was forbidden. If/when somebody was caught reading a Hebrew text, he/she was put in jail.

Of course, the numbers presented say a lot without the need for uttering additional word. There is even a custom to say, better than in numbers, nothing can be expressed. That is true, but still, the indescribable barbarian facts make any human being tremble when he/she reads of those events. The numbers remain dry and play only a complementary role in the entire picture. This is the reason behind our decision to present an event described, I would call firsthand, since by chance, we knew a nephew of the child whose story follows.

In czarist Russia, each Jewish community was forced, by law, to provide a number of children for the Russian state. Those children were taken from their homes, sent great distances, and raised in military units. Never again could such a child see his family. First of all, they were converted and their name changed. Then, during military campaigns, in the bloodiest battles, they were used.

The Jewish mothers were out of their minds when they had to give away their offsprings. Any possible means were used to save them. One method was to find a man able to carry one or two children and who would go from city to city, town to town, up to the Nistru River located at the border between Russia and Basarabia (a Romanian province from time to time, since the Russian policy was always to expand its borders). After this, during the night, taking each child under one of his arms, he had to pass the river. The understanding between mother and smuggler was clear: If the child became scared and started to cry, at the first uttered sound he would be drowned. This understanding was paid with a lot of money that had to be provided in advance. The Russian man had the duty to hand over the child to a Jewish family.

The grandchild of one such child smuggled over the mentioned river passed away several years ago in old age. His daughter lives in New Jersey. The brother of that child was scared during the operation, and he started to scream. The smuggler put the child's head into the water and everything was quiet again. The surviving child was taken in by a Jewish community that took care of his shelter and education.

We would like to mention that the author's great-grandfather, from his mother's side, was forced to leave his parents at the age of thirteen in order to save his life and his national identity. These were the conditions, or in other words the "great freedom," with which the Jews had to manage to educate themselves in order to maintain a certain human dignity in the process of survival. Having at their side only the eternal Book of Books, they succeeded in remaining alive.

After nineteen centuries of wanderings, beatings, and being pushed from one corner to the other of our common terra, through new sacrifices with new Jewish blood, they paved the way back to their ancestral country, their home devastated by all kinds of adventurers. Here again, their right is denied by conquerors and murderers, who came to wipe out any trace of Jewish life. Well known are the pogroms organized inside the Jewish Holy Land by those bandits, who even in our day are trying to demonstrate by lip science their superior right to that piece of land. They want to teach the Jewish people their history. King David was their ancestor, then Jerusalem wasn't the capital of the Jewish state, and anyway the Jews lost their true faith of Abraham, Isaac, and Jacob, and therefore their right does not exist.

Those funny guys forgot a very important fact: If someone is born in my house, my house doesn't become his property. A lot of children were and are born inside the New York City subway. According to that argument, the New York City subway has to become their property and they are entitled to own it and behave accordingly. In addition to all mentioned facts, their most holy right regarding Jerusalem consists in Mohammad's visit to the city, after his death, when he started the journey to heaven exactly from the place where the altar of the Jewish Temple was built. On their ancient soil, surrounded by bloody enemies, the Jews took charge in all departments of a civilized nation. Using the three distinct divisions in a state, legislative, executive, and judiciary, a democratic system of government has been created. We would dare say that many great states have much to learn from it. With a gun in one hand, and their eternal book in the other, the Israelis watch the precious jewel which they have regained: the spiritual, moral, and political freedom, together with a real and national independence on a chip of the ancient Israeli territory.

Five

There are circumstances in which I believe the use of force is appropriate namely, in the face of an enemy bent on destroying me and my people.

— A. Einstein

(A response to the criticism of a Japanese journal reproaching him for his involvement in World War II).

Chapter 5

Judaism, State and Zionism

5.1

Introduction

We have had occasion, up to now, to become acquainted with some ethical-moral elements of Judaism, as well as with the importance of truth in playing a crucial role in the entire Judaic system. Indeed, according to the basic Jewish laws, the following rules render the world:

i) Truth—Taking into account the basics of the Jewish faith, whose foundation is based on the essence of the Mosaic Law, the rabbis pointed out why this is the most important principle of the world. They tried to explain it in a manner accessible to each social layer of their community; this is why some additional hints are given.

The Hebrew word for truth is emeth which, written in Hebrew, contains three letters which are located at the beginning, at the middle, and at the end of the Hebrew alphabet. Just in the same way truth is beginning, the middle, and the end of our civilization. Truth is the seal of God; and, indeed, for a scientist a true law is for him a seal of nature, since each natural law follows its way for all mankind.

ii) Justice—Certain laws must be obeyed by each member of the considered society. It is the ideal that society can reach using some rules in a given moment of certain socioeconomic conditions.

iii) Peace—Israel's mission is peace, and the Jewish prayer reads: "Enable Israel to be a messenger of peace to the peoples of the Earth." Only during peacetime can the human society be developed; only during peacetime can all forces of a society be concentrated toward progress and well-being for all its members.

We want to reach some other facets which have a direct connection with an organized human collectivity. In the last three chapters, we reached important domains of Jewish legislation used to organize a human collectivity, as well as other legislations having the same purpose elaborated in antiquity. However our desire is to debate, and sometimes to develop briefly, the use of the same laws in specific given conditions. Since each social element belongs to a certain organized group, we are going to consider here also:

- The Jewish faith
- The state, purposes, functions
- Judaism, Christianity, Islam
- Foreign dominations of the Promised Land
- Aspects regarding the Jewish national rebirth on a

submicroscopic surface of their unquestionable ancient territory. In our opinion it is a "must" to consider here the above subjects; we do not want to leave even the slightest impression that we are avoiding or circumventing any phase regarding the theme of our book.

5.2

The Jewish Religion and Its Critics

We will try to point out here, in a more explicit way, an aspect that religion has to face in general, namely: is religion predestined to vanish? Some critics of the subject who consider themselves rationalists have started a systematic attack against religion in general. Confronted with an enemy whom you want to defeat, a tactic and strategy has to be developed according to the territory that is under his control. Since our surface area is located on a philosophical ground, the immediate requirement was to define religion: the enemy itself.

We suppose the reader has guessed already that in our era Karl Marx was the "general" in charge, aligning his philosophical "troops," giving first the following definition: Religion is the fantastic reflection of nature in the human mind, it is opium for the people. Second, any creation of the human mind took place on a certain rung of the development of humanity and, having a historical character, it must vanish on another superior rung of its development.

To give more credibility to this kind of argument, Marx and his followers studied the life and customs of some human collectivities that were on a low level of development, at least from a spiritual point of view. For instance, it could be observed that among some Lapps was a usual practice to worship the wind, the snow, and other natural phenomena. Based on such observations, Karl Marx drew the indisputable conclusion, "checked by practice". And since practice is the criterion of truth (section 1.2), everything seemed, at least for his followers, near perfection.

Of course, that fierce attack was first against the Hebrew Bible, since the ethics of the entire civilized world is based on its axioms. In order to get closure to facts, we are obliged first to make a trip to some archeological findings in that part of the world which seems to have cradled the main part of human population in the early stages. There, we can find proof that the ever-thinking man tried to know primarily his piece of land from which the much needed food was taken, and to ensure the security of his shelter. Our forefathers studied the natural phenomena on which they depended, as well as the health of their own bodies and of those close to them, etc. During that primitive true research, their imaginations started to contribute more and more to the progress of fellow men from that area.

First, the Sumerians (4000-3000 B.C.) of non-Semitic descent, later the Semitic populations located in the piece of land called Mesopotamia (2450-3000 B.C.), started to give special importance to the order of different things and phenomena. This is why in that part of the world, which was also the home of the Babylonians, Chaldeans, and Assyrians, all of Semitic descent, the order in their daily affairs was considered an inseparable part of their existence. (See for instance Sabatino Moscati, Le antice civieta semitice 1958, Gius. Laterza & Figli, s.p.a., casa editrice, Bari.) This may explain the well-known fact that in the specified area civilizations developed by taking over first the findings of the predecessor inhabitants, and enriching them by new, important, original results. They started to organize their life elaborating different activities inside a slave society.

Some critics, trying to attenuate the dazzling aspect of Moses' name, inseparable from his laws, suggested that these laws are in fact, a plagiarism. As a supreme argument, Hammurabi's Code, considered by those critics as being the oldest, is usually quoted. We mentioned Hamurabi's laws in section 3.2, but we didn't go into details considered unnecessary in that section.

First of all, there is an older code, by approximately two centuries, written in the Akkadian language and called Eshnuna's Code (according to the present data available, the Semites penetrated Mesopotamia throughout the Akkadian dynasty). Secondly, there is another code, contemporary with Eshnuna's Code, called the Lipit Istar Code (the princeps of Isin), which is written in the Sumerian language. Thirdly, there is still another code, called the Code of Ur-Nammu, older than the others, and written in the Sumerian language approximately 2050 B.C.

From a comparative study of those codes, it seems that the main importance of the legislation set up by Hammurabi consisted first in the fact that he took over the previous tradition and unified those laws. In addition, he applied the unified laws on a large scale inside the late Mesopotamian society and succeeded in imposing his legislation even beyond that area. According to the semitic point of view regarding order, Hammurabi introduced new elements too, that in a way represent a kind of Lex Talionis. We underscore, "a kind of Lex Talionis," because in the system of social organization of Hammurabi's state, it was a powerful social discrepancy. This law means an eye for an eye and a tooth for a tooth. But the law could be applied only to members belonging to the same social layers. According to Moses' legislation, the law was applied in the same way to all members of the social body, absolutely without exception.

Second, the Jewish Code has been ameliorated by the fact that equivalent punishments were introduced. In Hammurabi's Code, the slaves were considered simple objects belonging to the owner, the only advantage of such a humiliating situation consisted in a minimum protection offered by the owner. It is a typical slavery code that organized and defended the slavery society. Indeed, if a slave left his owner, he was forced to come back and be punished accordingly for breaking the law. As I specified earlier, according to Moses' Law, if a slave left his owner's house, he was considered a free man. This is a clear example of how Moses tried to abolish slavery, which he considered a shame of the human race, but in the given conditions, such a radical change could not be done at once. This is why he specified in the given law regarding the subject: after serving seven years, any slave must be freed. If/when a slave refuses his/her freedom, then he/she has to be punished. The punishment by itself was a mild one. It consisted mainly of a kind of earring that showed that the wearer refused one of the most precious things of a human being — freedom.

As we mentioned already (in section 2.8), the smallest injury to the body of a slave, when working for his owner, made him a free man (Exodus 21:26-27). It is no secret that Moses elaborated his entire legislation based on the axioms of Judaism with their ever-shining spark, whose light became more and more stimulated during its triumphant way throughout history. It looks like the eternal fire seen by Moses when he met the Almighty in the wilderness for the first time via the burning bush, without being consumed. That kind of eternal inspiration represents a permanent lively guide giving the human element the possibility of living in a civilized society (see also 3.2). The Hebrew Bible does not consider the human social body like something cast forever. The basics of Moses' Law have been detached from the multitude of natural phenomena, containing in its structure the everlasting youth with endless life. As we already know, a physical law never vanishes. In time, that law may become a particular case of a more general one, but its domain of validity remains unchanged.

Therefore, again, using the analogy of the branch of strong science called physics, virtually all of Marx's arguments regarding Moses' Laws are smashed. But any adopted law, in any stage of social development, must remain valid when it is passed through the spinning nozzle of the postulates. This principle, well known in science, was introduced by Albert Einstein in 1905. Since Marx died much earlier, he was convinced that by blaming Moses he would reach the same "altitude" in giving a different ethics in order to organize a brand new society.

5.3

The State and Some Socio-Ethical Aspects

According to social conventions established by historical conditions among communities related by the same local ancestors, united in their common fight for existence, there came into being, the social organization called the state. Finally there is a body of people occupying a definite territory, organized from a certain point of view, under a certain administrative apparatus, known in our day as "government." During the process of its gestation, two concepts were born: the concept of the moral and its opposite, the immoral. Any one of them may use the other as a frame of reference. Since the moral constitutes the predominant concept, it results that the other one is in disgrace inside the given state, being in, essence, condemned by the majority of the considered social body.

Since in some cases, it is difficult for different social elements to distinguish one from the other, rules of behavior were introduced; first in small communities and then gradually extending to the groups of common ancestors. Thus, a state must be an organized body, as specified above, having as a special aim to supervise and control the established rules in order to be respected by all members of the considered community. Of course, these rules are exercised in an area occupied by people of common ancestry as well as by some other people of different ancestry, living in that area and constituting a minority group. To supervise and judge different violations from the established norms, the state needs a special apparatus. Some like to call it an apparatus of constraint, we prefer to call it a useful social device to avoid social chaos, by respecting the law in a given framework.

From here, two main functions result:

i) An internal one that regards the suppression of perturbations eventually produced by some social elements because of different violations of established social conventions.

ii) An external one that has as a main purpose to establish and maintain relations with other states while creating a means to guard the territorial integrity of the state and the welfare of its inhabitants.

Therefore, each state must have a legislative power and an executive power.

In time, the evolution of different states became diverse. Taking into account how the states are organized, we may classify them in the following way: totalitarian, semi-democratic, and democratic (we call democratic one which practices social equality).

To complete the "painting" of what we just presented, we must add some words regarding politics, since each state is using a way of regulating its own affairs. The assembling of the means needed to maintain and develop the economy of a state, form and determine its wisdom in the management on internal and external level, and finally become concretized is what we call politics. We emphasize the fact that the politics does not represent necessarily the interest of the entire population of a given country; sometimes it represents only the interests of a group, or some groups, that are defending only their situation and through different manipulations they succeed, at least for a while, in controlling the entire social body.

The Jewish religion was born before the Jewish state; in the midst of the desert where the slaves of yesterday organized themselves into twelve tribes and were armed with the necessary theoretical elements to organize their future state based on complete new principles, compared with all contemporary states. There, in the wilderness, they received the ethical norms with their timeless youth because of the embedded invariant grain that is, in our day, associated with the Jewish people. The Torah helped the Jews to survive and, since the backbone of the Torah consists on the axioms of Judaism, we may say that we are truly anchored to them, body and soul. This is a fact that cannot be denied.

For instance, the well-known French philosopher and rationalist Voltaire used to say, between the Jews and God there is a special "love affair." This is the right time to define the Jewish religion, since the reader has to know where we stand. The Judaic religion is a system of social organization, a benevolent self-control of individual life inside the human society. Such a behavior corresponds to a human internal necessity, to man's essence, to prove how he, as a human being, can differentiate himself from the rest of the animal world. It teaches us how to deal with our fellow man as well as with the supreme parameter, the everlasting Creator. The Mosaic revolutionary thinking was a novelty not only for those men, who lived as slaves for centuries, but for every other free man of that epoch.

As an example, we may quote Aristotle, the great Greek philosopher who lived approximately a millennium later. He said, "It is impossible for me even to imagine how a society without slavery would look!"

But Moses wasn't only a theoretician; he was a practical man, too. He understood the necessity for his people to be completely detached not only from the previous life but from everything that was going on in the surrounding world. He kept the Jews in the wilderness in order to instruct and educate a new generation of free men. Without such a vision, his entire project could fail. During forty years, the older generation could have little or no influence at all. He formed a young new army with an open soul and mind, imbued by the new conception of what is right and what is wrong. In front of such a military organization of free men, well aware of what they are fighting for and their mission as a chosen people, nothing could hinder or stop them.

From the pages of the Hebrew Bible, one can see how the Jewish fighters tried to spare human lives, but when the opponents didn't give up, they subdued them by force. It has been observed that the psychological structure of a normal human is made up in such a way that an evolved religious system serves him as a guide to peace with himself, and prompts him to look around and see whenever another man needs his help, regardless of what that man believes or worships.[1] Judaism has nothing to do with partisans of any religion that has as a purpose, the propagation of their religion or its imposition by force. On the contrary, orthodox Jewish teaching forbids the recruitment of converts. According to Jewish writings, peace will be spread on the surface of the Earth when the worship of idolatry will cease. Of course, if the seven obligations that exist for Noah's descendants are respected (sec. 4.3), then peace can be installed in every corner of the Earth.

---

[1] We say that a religious system is evolved if/when during the centuries and millennia it could be verified as being in full accord with well-known scientific facts.

5.4

Zion and the Jewish Soul

The name Zion, has for each Jew who received his basic knowledge regarding the Hebrew Bible at a traditional Jewish school, a very special resonance. Maybe not each one of the mentioned people would be able to explain in detail the meaning of this word, but he/she will never remain silent when the name will reach his/her audible system. I remember when, many years ago, an Israeli children ensemble of dancers and singers visited my native country, which was then under Communist rule. I was present, together with my wife. It was an auditorium for approximately three thousand spectators, and it was full. No chair remained vacant. The chorus started to sing, "Jerushalaim." When the word Jerushalaim was heard, to my surprise, every Jewish person forgot where he was. He forgot even the simple fact that there might be some secret agents nearby and that the next day his job might be in jeopardy. Thousands of hands started to applaud. It was an instinctive spontaneous behavior, since Jerusalem symbolizes the spiritual heart and soul of the Jewish people. Only a representative of Lebanon who was present to report the atmosphere left nervously. Every time the name came up, everything was repeated. Some among those present, a number of whom we knew, had a very poor Jewish education; we doubted some others who had any background regarding Judaism, but they were Jews, and at the name of Jerushalaim, a chord of their heart was plucked.

As a result of the physical phenomenon called resonance, they answered by applauding.

But we start to talk about Zion and we want to answer first the question: from where did the name come from? One of the mountains of Jerusalem is called Zion and on that mountain the arc of alliance of the twelve Israelite tribes, symbol of national and religious unity, was brought and located approximately three thousand years ago. Therefore, the name of Zion responds to the Judaic psychological chords stretched at maximum by almost two millennia of diaspora, suffering, and persecution. Section 4.7 showed only a pale image of Jewish oppression. The name of Zion answers to the echo that the name Jerusalem has in every Jewish heart. Jerusalem, where they were forbidden to come and settle or visit, their house, their country, their Promised Land, the graves of their forefathers, their kings, prophets, and the Western Wall crying on the ruins of their Temple, their lost country.[2]

The wall is a remnant of the first house built to worship the unique parameter that governs the entire universe. However, risking their lives, they came here all the time, poor and rich, from each corner of the earth, and some of them succeeded even in settling in their robbed house, bribing the local authorities. The number of settled Jews varied greatly as a function of the given historical conditions. Starting with the year 70, the Jews lost even their political autonomy. Up to 1948, when the modern State of Israel was recognized, there had been 1,878 years of continuous foreign domination and destruction, as well as border changes dictated by different political administrative manipulations of

---

[2] By the fourth century, Jews were allowed to come only on Tisha Be'av, when they would cry over their destruction. Hence, it was derisively called by some non Jews "the Wall of Weeping", "the Wall of Tears" or "the Wailing Wall." In the nineteenth century, Jews had to pay to pray here; in 1887, Baron Rothschild tried to buy it, but Turkey (who was the ruler) said no.

the occupiers. Then, on a literally submicronic part of the ancient Jewish territory, some of the survivors of the Holocaust could finally find a home and rebuild their shattered lives. In order to give an image of the agitated history in that place, we present the following list of the conquerors who succeeded one another after the uprising of Bar-Kohba in A.D. 70.

Domination	Years
Roman	70
Byzantine	315-636
Arab	636-1072
Seldjugs	1072-1099
Crusaders	1099-1291
Mameluke	1291-1516
Turkish	1516-1917
English	1918-1948

Every occupant brought in new changes dictated by the purpose and necessities of the new power. Thus, the Romans changed the name of the Jewish country, calling it Palestine, trying in this way to erase any trace of any right or heritage regarding the Jewish state. The new name had been taken from a small population, which had some time in the past inhabitated a small coastal strip known today as the Gaza Strip. They were called Philistines. (In modern times, we understand this name to mean somebody who is hostile or indifferent to culture, commonplace, prosaic. The understanding of this meaning is perhaps taken from the fact that King David, a poet, a man who fought for culture, defeated the Philistine Goliath, who represented brutal force.)

The Romans moved further with their manipulations, changing the name of Jerusalem, the Jewish eternal capital, to Aelia Capitolina. The more than three million Jews who inhabitated the country, according to estimates of that time, were exiled and many of them sold as slaves. Others where killed. The Jews remained, as far as they could, in the Middle East and around the Mediterranean Basin, being on the watch to find a favorable moment to return to their homeland. They risked their lives and all their belongings in order to feel again under their feet, the ancestral ground. In this way, the Jews succeeded for a while to maintain a Jewish majority.

Only during the Byzantine occupation were the Jewish elements driven out by draconic measures and Christians were brought in. Only, in this way, their number was exceeded by non-Jews. However, the Roman and Byzantine dominations are characterized by survival of the Jewish community, which was particularly dense in Galilee, the valleys, on the coast, and in Judea. Their spiritual life continued to be intense in spite of the adverse conditions. The major achievements during the mentioned period are: The Mishna, completed during the second century, and the Jerusalem Talmud, which was accomplished between the fourth and fifth centuries (see appendix D).

When, in the year 636, the Arab armies, as carriers of Muhammad's new religion, armed to the teeth in order to impose their belief by the sword, occupied the Jewish territory, they found many Jewish villages. The inhabitants of those villages were converted to Islam by force. Those who refused were killed. Others fled, leaving everything to the occupants in order to save their lives. The Jews offered fierce resistance, but they were no match for the conqueror's army of an endless number of fighters. Within a few centuries, the Jews were driven out of the countryside, and the land became Arab property.

The Arabs have a special point of view regarding the ownership of a field suitable for farming. If one is a landowner, then he considers himself as belonging to a special high class. We learned this after visiting some Arab villages; it gave us a new understanding regarding their attitude through history. Under these conditions, the entire Jewish population became concentrated in cities for almost a millennium. The main centers of Jewish life were in Jerusalem, Tiberias, Safed, and Hebron. Beside the fact that the Arabs totally abolished by force the Jewish ownership of land, they divided the Jewish territory into two military districts separated by the Jordan River, calling them Palestine and Jordan. We can see again the same tendency as the Romans had, not to remind anything of the Jewish state, even though in their religion are many elements taken from the Hebrew Bible, including Abraham, Isaac, and Jacob, as well as the clear specification as to whom the mentioned territories belong.[3]

During the Crusades, the Arabs were in as great a danger of being killed as the Jews. Then, and only then, Jews and Arabs fought shoulder to shoulder in order to save their lives. The Crusaders did not significantly change the population's character since their number was small. Indeed they never exceeded 30,000 men. Their remarkable achievements consisted in the destruction of the cities and villages, as well as the depopulating of the coastline that remained in that unchanged state up to the second half of the nineteenth century when the organized Jewish emigration started.

During the Mameluke domination, the country was divided into three administrative districts: Safed, Gaza, Damask. The occupiers didn't give any name to the country robbed from the Jews. Under the Turkish administration, a regime of insecurity and oppression had been installed

---

[3] Muslim, Jewish, and Christian scriptures agree that the "West Bank" Golan Heights, Gaza, East Jerusalem as well as Israel proper belong to the Jews. The Muslim scripture, the Koran, clearly states that Allah assigned the Holy Land to the Jews (Sura V, "The Table"). But a robber does not believe in anything. This is why the wanderers of the Arab world claim it from Israel. Are they fundamentalists or ordinary robbers?

throughout the country of Israel. Different Arab tribes started to infiltrate the Jewish territory in order to rob the local population. Internal fights took place at the level of local alliances. As a result, the number of cities decreased, and the population did too.

In the second half of the nineteenth century, the Jewish and Arab communities started to increase. The Jews started to move in increasing number toward the Promised Land with the help of the other brothers from the diaspora. With the system of communications being improved, help could be sent much faster where and when needed. Nobody protected the life of the Jewish population. They were in continuous danger, since the Arab adventurers from the neighboring countries looked at the influx of Jewish people with more than an unfriendly eye. Indeed, as a result, they started to infiltrate with the special purpose of preventing the Jews from becoming a majority. One of the most important jobs performed by the infiltrants was first of all to rob the Jewish population. This kind of action had a double purpose:

- To give the Arab adventurers the necessary means to start a new life in foreign territory.
- To persuade the Jews to leave by intimidation.

The Turks divided the country into administrative districts and did not give any special name to the land that would be designated the Jewish country. The English domination that followed maintained the name of Palestine given by the Romans to the historical Jewish territory. The British Empire had a mandate over a surface area of 120,000 square km. The surface area included both sides of the Jordan River and the Golan Heights. This was incomparably less than the Jewish heritage; however, it included that part of the country where, from a historical point of view, the main events took place regarding the Jewish and Christian tradition.

Interested from a purely political point of view, as well as the smell of gasoline which they started to like, the British, in 1921, divided the mandated area under jurisdiction, an already well-mutilated Jewish territory, into two parts: Palestine and Jordan (the Golan being given to the French, the big boss of Syria at that time). The first one on the west bank of the Jordan River and the other on the east bank. When you have at your disposal, the territory of a people spread out in all corners of our terra, it is easy for a mighty power, without paying anything, to move its pencil on the map and change the borders of that people's land. Winston Churchill used to say, "I created Transjordan with a stroke of a pen on a Sunday afternoon in Cairo."

Therefore, from the beginning, the new Jewish hope was robbed by treacherous maneuvers. In addition, the long-term plan of the British Empire included the necessity to maintain ownership of the Suez Canal, and Jordan was a good base for them. Of course, the Sinai Desert could be used for such a defensive purpose, but then, serious investments were needed. According to British calculations, the Jews could not be trusted if a conflict broke out. Then, with one bullet, the British tried to shoot two rabbits:

• To please the surrounding population by the creation of a new Arab kingdom, at Jewish expense, in which everything was under their control.

• To prepare a military base with a minimum of investment, the special purpose of which was to defend the Suez Canal.

The first was extremely easy to accomplish, since an Arab prince willing to ascend the throne could always be found without difficulty. This brief description constitutes the historical base for the Jordanian state and the "indubitable rights" of the so-called Palestinian adventurers: the theft from the Jewish national patrimony carried out under the benevolent eye of the

British administration. The international Jewish communities had always sent financial help to rebuild the Jewish homeland destroyed by diverse invaders over the centuries. In these conditions, it was obvious that the life of the Jewish farmers was different from that of the Arab farmers located in the neighboring countries.

From the newspapers of that time, one can learn about the visits organized by the British administration of Arab groups from limitrophe countries to different Jewish settlements. The result of such exchanges were Arab armed attacks on the Jewish settlements for the special purpose of robbing and destroying. In the meantime, Jewish emigration, mainly from Europe, was obstructed in all possible ways, while the Arab migration toward the Holy Land was stimulated.

We have to mention that, to the credit of the British people, among the ranks of the British army were officers who knew that the balance was inclined in an abusive way toward those who had no right whatsoever, and they acted accordingly. They did it without any hope of reward; on the contrary, their social position and freedom were at stake. Among the simple British soldiers, as well as the civil employees, voices were raised in defense of the people of the Hebrew Bible. By an irony of fate, the most knowledgeable people about the uneasy history of the Jews, their exile in order to defend their belief in the unique and invisible God, and their historical indisputable rights regarding the Holy Land raised all kind of hindrances in the way of their return. The nostalgia was powerful. During our lectures in the Jewish school, we could see, we would dare to say almost touch with the imagination, our ancient land as well as those who didn't allow us to rebuild the totally neglected country. None of the invading hordes was interested in the maintenance of different places which were both close to the

Jewish soul and we would dare to say, important for the entire civilized population of our planet. We believe without the Jewish scriptures and the Jewish people striving throughout history to survive, the Christian Church as well as the Islamic religion would not exist.

5.5

Arabs, Muslims and Civilization

The Hebrew Bible isn't only the base of our faith and ethics, but it constitutes a unique document showing the exclusive right of the Jewish people regarding their homeland. No other people in this world are able to present written proof to sustain its rights. Therefore, we consider it important to present this aspect, too, since the Hebrew Bible is venerated by approximately half the people on our planet, while they neglect, almost completely, the justified Jewish claim.

This is why after providing the scientific structure of Jewish Book of Books, as well as other essential aspects, we must mention and claim the exclusive ownership of our ancestral land. In order to help everybody understand that we are extremely modest in our demands, a little extra history is necessary. Those who deny our historical rights regarding the Jewish ancestral home are those who did not respect even their holy book, the Koran, and they are daring to call themselves Arabs.

But who are they? The Arabs (not the adventurers of the Middle East) are a people of Semitic descent, originally living exclusively in that vast territory called Arabia proper (with the Hedjaz), Yemen, Oman, and some smaller countries, a subcontinent rather than a country, covering millions of square kilometers. From the town of Hedjaz, the great Islamic movement originated approximately 1,500 years ago. With the irresistible force of a primitive, uncorrupted people, of a stirring new faith, and of the fanaticism of men to whom death in battle to spread Muhammad's law by sword was the eternal joy, the Arabs overran neighboring countries and established dependent states. The population of the new states had to adopt the Islamic religion, and since their holy book, the Koran, is written in Arabic, with few exceptions, they generally adopted the language too, but not the civilization and culture, which was inferior to their own. Indeed, the great civilization developed in the following centuries in centers like Cordoba, Baghdad, Cairo, and Damascus was that of Arabic-speaking Muslims of varied races, but not an Arab civilization. A simple proof of our assertion constitutes the fact that Arabia itself, the cradle of the new faith, remained completely outside of the mentioned spiritual development.

5.6

The Owners of Palestine and the Jews

Islam, the religion founded by Mohammed, recognizes Moses' books, the Jewish prophets, and the Christian Gospels as an expression, though corruptly transmitted, of the Divine Will, and ranks Moses and Jesus among the prophets, the most important being Mohammed. It may have been expected that the contact of Islam with the Jewish territory (they call it Palestine), the land of both elder religions, would have resulted in an extraordinary spiritual and cultural development, that the confessors of Islam would have tried to justify their claim to religious superiority by great spiritual efforts. But the land became barren under their administration, and the conquerors were no tillers. They did not even try to develop anything like a Palestinian civilization.

The only remarkable monument of their reign was one already mentioned, the greatest profanation known in history, the construction of the Dome of the Rock, or Mosque of Omar, on the Mount Temple, exactly where the altar was located in the Jewish temple, the first building in the world raised as a house of prayer for the abstract invisible God. Although the construction of the mosque was commissioned by Arabs, in fact it was the work of Greek architects and artificers (see Sir

---

[4] After East Jerusalem was liberated during the 1967 war by the Israeli army, we could find in newspapers the laughable claim of some Muslim adventurers of the Middle East that their families lived for 1,500 years continuously in that city. We are still surprised they did not claim yet that King David was their ancestor.

Flinders Petrie, "The Revival of Palestine" pamphlet, p. 3).

The so-called Palestine has never had more than a thin layer of Arab population, and only 437 years of Arab rule during more than three thousand years of recorded history. For a relatively short time (636-1072) after the Arab conquest, which took place more than twelve centuries ago, the country was subjected to foreign Islamic rulers and a ruling class of Arabs. Eventually the country was conquered as specified in sections 5.4 and 5.5, and subjugated by various peoples such as the Seldjugs, the Kurds, the Mamelukes (a cast composed of Circassian slaves), the Crusaders, and finally by the Ottoman Turks. But never after the year 1072 has Arab rule existed in the so-called Palestine.

When in 1099, the Crusaders took Jerusalem, they massacred the entire Muslim population of about 70,000 people: all of new changes were marked by similar totalitarian measures.[4] The whole history of the territory called Palestine is an almost uninterrupted story of wanton destruction of human life and property. At the end of the eighteenth century, the land was practically empty. Thus, the French traveler Volney, who visited the country in 1783-85, characterized Palestine as one of the most devastated parts of Syria and speaks of the general decay of the country (Volney, Voyage en Syrie at Egypte, vol.2, Paris: 1787, p. 303, 313).

J.S. Buckingham, who visited the country in 1816, states that Jaffa "has all the appearances of a poor village, and every part of it that we saw was of corresponding meanness." In Rihhah, he found the work done by women and children; "the men roam the plains on horse-back, and live by robbery and plunder, which form their chief and most gainful occupation" (J.S. Buckingham, Travels in Palestine, London: 1821, p. 146, 302). A German encyclopedia published in 1827 calls Palestine "desolate and roamed through by Arab bands of robbers

(Brockhaus, Allg. deutche Real-Encyclopedie, 7 Aufl. Leipzig: 1827, "verodoet and arabishen Rauberbandend durehstreift" (vol 8). In 1833, Colonel Conder called Palestine "a ruined land" (Conder, Heth and Moab, London: 1833, p.380). A traveler, S. Olin, in 1840 is a valuable witness, since he was an admirer of the so-called Palestinian (Syrian) population, calling it "a fine-spirited race of men" and ridicules the idea of Jewish colonization (S. Olin, Travels in Egypt, Arabia Petraea and the Holy Land, vol. 2, New York: 1843, p.438, 439, 77, 88). According to him, the population was in decline. In Hebron "many houses are in a dilapidated state and uninhabitated;" the once populated region between Hebron and Bethlehem "is now abandoned and desolate" and has "dilapidated towns."

During the nineteenth century the Turkish government settled Bosnians, Turkomans, and after 1883, Circassians there. Thus, at least 25 percent of those 141,000 who were settled in Palestine in 1882 were newcomers or descendants of those who arrived after the Egyptian conquest. Consequently, in 1882, no more than about 106,000 settled Muslims had more than fifty years connection with the country. This was the situation when the Jews began to repopulate their destroyed country in an organized way.

In 1882, the first agricultural settlements were built, and in 1909, the foundations for the city of Tel-Aviv were laid. By 1895 there were 252,000 settled Muslims. By infiltration from neighboring countries, the Muslim population started to grow. The country was confronted for the first time with a large immigration of Arabic-speaking people which coincided with the development of Jewish settlements. For instance, *The Handbook of Palestine* by Luke and Keth-Roach (3rd edition, 1934), speaks of the "continuous replenishment of Palestine and Syria from the tribes of the Arabian desert" (p. 41). In 1935, the British Mandates Commission discussed a declaration of the governor of the Syrian Hauran district that in 1934, within a few months, 30,000 Houranese had entered Palestine and settled there (Minutes of the British Permanent Mandates Commission, 27th session, 1935, p.47).

All the presented facts show clearly that the genuine Arabs of Palestine are, in great majority, newcomers. Their invasion of the ancestral Jewish territory (by some Muslim adventurers) became attractive only when the organized Jewish colonization started. All the above-mentioned facts constitute the holy rights of the so-called Palestinian people. These are the people who profaned in Hebron the burial site of Abraham and Sarah, Issac and Rebecah, Jacob and Leah, the founders of the Jewish people, by building a mosque there, and forbidding the Jews to visit the ancestral graves. In 1929, they massacred or put to flight, the entire Jewish population of Hebron.

5.7

Zion and Diaspora

In section 4.5, we tried to present some aspects of the spiritual food of the Jew starting with his/her early childhood. As soon as he started to speak and could learn a prayer, he knew to turn his face toward Jerusalem. During the celebration of Passover, the closing part of the ceremony included the wish, and is still the same, "Next year in Jerusalem." The education of the Jewish child in the religious school and within his family was usually completed outside the school by the hatred against him experienced in the street, during his outdoor games, and later during his military service. Even during wartime, when as a devoted citizen he came to defend his home country at the risk of his life, praying according to his religion for the victory of the army whose member he was, it didn't matter; because first of all he was Jewish, and then discrimination against him had to be used.

The emancipation brought new disappointments for the Jew. The people continued to endure painful experiences. Their minds were tortured to find a way that would guide them in solving the problem of Jewish identity. As a result, between 1860 and 1890, some new ideas were published. The first work having such a theme, by Moses Hess, was titled, *Rome and Jerusalem*, published in 1862. The author pleaded for a return of the Jewish People to their ancestral country from whence they were forced out, and for the creation of a spiritual center for diaspora Judaism.

The ideas published by Hess were taken over and refined by Peretz Smolenski (1842-1885), who left his native Russia for Vienna, where he set up a monthly literary publication in Hebrew. Here he published an essay, "The Eternal People", which underscored the fact that the Jews were a nation of intellectuals which used the Hebrew language. The conclusion was that the Jewish intellectual values, the Jewish genius, would be able to flourish again inside the ancestral land.

Rabbi Samuel Mohilever (1824-1898), launched the first wave of organized emigration toward the Promised Land, founding an organization, "The Lovers of Zion." This organization found later one of the most capable leaders in the person of Judah Pinsker (1821-1891), previously a medical officer in the ranks of the czarist Russian army. After his friends were killed in an anti-Jewish pogrom in Odessa, Pinsker denounced the assimilation as a useless anti-Semite slogan. The organized movement born as a result of such activities, having as its purpose the national liberation of the Jewish people from oppression, received the symbolic name Zionism. Therefore, the present name is a new one given to an old ideology that has the same age as the Jewish arrival into the Promised Land.

From this, we can see that a change takes place simultaneously, with the transformation of the anti-Jewish medieval current into the anti-Semitism and racism of the modern epoch. The Jewish movements represented a huge step forward; however, they did not provide a program that could be viewed as a long-term methodical plan for a national rebirth in the borders of the Jewish ancestral land.

The roads needed to conduct the Jewish people to their indisputable ancestral home were elaborated by Theodore Herzl (1860-1904), the founder of modern scientific Zionism. His masterpiece, *The Jewish State,* published in 1896, caused a sensation among his contemporaries. Using the Zionist ideal,

Theodore Herzl showed a clear way toward Zion, the symbol of national unity. Using with great skill the elements of the scientific method (see 1.2) to find a solution for a thorny problem, Theodore Herzl succeeded in convoking, in 1897, the first Zionist Congress in Basel where the creation of the "World Zionist Organization," as well as the creation of a Jewish state on the ancestral Israelite territory, were approved.

In his approach, Zionism represented a movement of different social layers of the Jewish population in different countries. It included eventually farmers, workers, leaders, entrepreneurs, owners, students, and intellectuals. All the specified social groups could feel the radiation of hope spread by the new doctrine, a genuine fire of national revival. Then Zionist organizations were created in all countries, where the Jewish youngsters were trained with the special purpose of beginning a new life under difficult conditions on the devastated areas of their ancestral land. The neglected soil was unproductive. The new emigrant had to fight with perseverance. He created terraces, moving soil from one place to another and even importing it when needed. It was a terrible fight. The international Jewry was behind them. All social layers pitched in, many times from very modest incomes. But their feeling for Zion was more important; their eyes shone at the name of Zion, and they wanted to feel in a way or another a participation in the great enterprise of rebuilding their country; the wonderful places of their untarnished diamond, the "Hebrew Bible."

After nineteen centuries of homelessness, wandering through the entire world, the spirit of sacrifice was high. Jewish students dropped out of universities in order to go and work, to dig and improve the fields of their patriarchs. Hope and experience were moving hand-in-hand; indeed inside the Zionist movement the people received a multilateral training. Youngsters of different backgrounds started being trained in an organized way by working in factories and in the fields, inside the organized teams called "halutzim." It was more than impressive to see highly qualified people working in domains that had nothing to do with their background, working hard to get new knowledge for themselves and to share their rich previous background with every member of the movement.

Although the Jews had to endure all kinds of unimaginable humiliations over the centuries, absolutely none of the Zionist organizations had in its program the slightest trace of national hatred. Things were pushed extremely far regarding this aspect. Thus, when some Arabs started a terror campaign by killing women, children, and men who could not defend themselves, the killers were not judged according to the "Lex Talionis Law" as they deserved. The Zionists felt that only on the battlefield did they have the right to kill the enemy. Taking into account such a behavior, we may suppose that the reader is able to draw a conclusion regarding the Zionists and the Zionist movement. According to their distinguished character, we may call them the noble gentlemen of sacrifice and hope of the Jewish people, their program being drawn from the conception of the Jewish forefathers regarding human society—a life of creation under the sign of truth and attachment to the values of mankind.

In order to underscore my previous statements, I would like to present the behavior of one of those "Sionists" on the battlefield.[5] He grew up in Romania, and at a young age he, together with his family, tried to reach the Jewish ancestral land still called at that time Palestine. In fact, he was on an illegal refugee ship that had been captured by the British, and spent time in an internment camp in Cyprus with his entire

---

5 The source of this short presentation of the described Israeli officer is the Jerusalem Post from June 18, 1999, written by Abraham Abramovici

family and a lot of other Jews who used the same route in order to reach their ancestral homeland. England of that time made a huge departure from the policy of the noble Englishman, Lord Arthur James Balfour (1848-1930), who became an ardent Zionist following two brief, but momentous encounters with Chaim Weizmann. The experience in Cyprus increased his taste for the sea. In Israel, as an adult, he chose the navy as his main occupation. He served on submarines for ten years. In 1971, he joined the missile boat flotilla. In July 1973, he was named commander of the missile flotilla. He brought here a new analytical approach and an exemplary operational discipline. As we know, shortly after this an attack was launched by Syria and Egypt during the holiest day of the Jewish calendar, on Yom Kippur. Only Nazi Germany could have made a similar choice.

On October 2, 1973, three months after assuming command, Michael Barkai led the flotilla out to sea for its first-ever full-scale rehearsal. Using his own innovations, from a "14-knots navy"—the cruising speed of the old destroyers in the past—it became now a 30-knots navy. He spent three days with his navy practicing the new tactics that had been developed for a new type of warfare. Michael Barkai played a key role in devising the new tactics where electronic beams and other new revolutionary systems had to be used. It was extremely important to work with great precision since at that time, just before the war broke out, the Soviet Union had just delivered the Styx missiles to the Arabs and those missiles had a range of 45 kilometers, compared with the Gabriel missiles that had a range of only 20 kilometers.

A Jewish naval wizard, Herut Tzemah, developed an electronic warfare system to divert the incoming Styx missiles using false signals, but everything could be tested only on the ground. An educated guess remains an educated guess until practice will confirm its validity. The man had to be released for Yom Kippur, October 5; however, an alert was announced and all leaves were canceled. The war broke out on Yom Kippur, Barkai had to clear the sea lanes, permitting vital supplies to get through. Then Barkai led a six-boat task north and shortly after dark they entered Syrian waters. He gave a clear order about their mission: The enemy has to be drawn out of Latakia, a main Syrian harbor. All educated guesses devised by Tzemah worked and the result was that all five enemy vessels were sent at the bottom of the sea. The battle of Latakia was the first ever known between two opposing missile boat formations without seeing each other; everything was based on radar information only. None of the Israeli vessels was hit by the enemy.

On their way back, Barkai's task force could see the balconies and the rooftops of Haifa crowded with spectators as they approached during the morning hours. Everybody already knew about their military victory. However, Michael Barkai ordered that brooms would not be tied to the vessels' masts in the traditional symbol of navy victory. He gave this order telling his officers that they had left a lot of Syrian sailors at the bottom of the sea, and any flaunting of victory "wouldn't be respectful to them or to ourselves." This was the behavior of a "Sionist" member of the Sionist Jewish army. These people were characterized as fascists by those who had indeed such a behavior.

Restless fighters for the historical rights of the Jewish people, they are active promoters of Judeo-Christian friendship, maintaining the distinct Jewish character according to the ancient Jewish tradition and, as we could see, scientific tradition too. Through their superhuman work, in a country brought to total ruin by its invaders, these men prepared the necessary means to abolish the Diaspora; in the meantime, they found material proofs regarding the Judaic roots of

Christianity. The sweat and blood of these noble youngsters contributed to dissipate the hypothesis of those historians who tried to connect Christianity with barbarian primitive customs. The sons and daughters of the Israeli people, fighters for justice and truth, brought their contribution even in this domain. In our opinion, the Christian church in general should support without hesitation these genuine noble defenders of truth and righteousness. In Europe, primarily in the Eastern part of Europe, the concepts born in the darkness of the medieval period about Jews and their religion still persist, even though they know that their Lord Jesus was Jewish. The Church was very stubborn in teaching the truth about the unity of the Judeo-Christian tradition that underlies the diversity of creed and ritual known to philosophers of the Middle Ages as well as by the scholars of Eastern Europe of our days.[6] These are the Zionists, men with golden hearts, nerves of steel, arms of iron, outstanding in character, based on the ethics of their heritage, tempered in battles and in anguish. The name of their movement indicates the historical religious framework in which they are anchored; namely, the material and cultural background and the old symbol of unity of the Jewish people from every corner of the terra.

In this sense, the Zionist movement constitutes the quintessence of what every Jew had dreamt for nineteen centuries, in all countries and continents of the Diaspora. Even when their enemies forced them out of their country, they had sworn they would be back, since this was not the first time in their tormented history that it had happened. For example, Psalm 137 refers to the exiled children of Israel, by the waters of Babylon:

"How shall we sing the Lord's song in a strange land?

---

[6] See also Jacob Bernard Agus, *The Evolution of Jewish Thought*, London: Abelard Schuman, 1959 p. 144

If I forget thee, O Jerusalem, let my right hand
forget her cunning.
If I do not remember thee, let my tongue cleave to the
roof of my mouth;
If I prefer not Jerusalem above my highest joys."

Therefore, to fight or even denigrate Zionism, a current of national revival among the people of the Hebrew Bible, the scientific bases of which have been presented; based on its outstanding content regarding the truth and justice in the world, such denigration constitutes not only a pure degrading racism, but an enmity directed against the most elementary human requirements. We cannot close the last chapter of this book before we remind and justify for our reader why different historical facts were included in our digest. We suppose that the facts are simple and clear: Jewish history indicates Jewish religion, and the Jewish religion underscores Jewish history.

Instead of Postface

Judaism seems to me to be concerned almost exclusively with the moral attitude in life and to life.

— A. Einstein.

Instead of Postface

We arrive at the end of this book, and we hope that the reader has been rewarded for his effort. However, we don't want to close the last pages without emphasizing the connection of the beginning of the Hebrew Bible (Moses' first book) with strong science as well as with some other aspects.

Indeed, the blank page of pre-Creation is handled accordingly. Using the specific language of that time, the interconnected results are presented rather in a concise, short form, providing an explanation of the beginning of the universe at the level of understanding of any human being. Science moved in much later, in order to prove and justify those explanations that sound like simple statements. For example, at the beginning it was chaos that science of our day considers to be true. Another is "and there was evening and there was morning, day one" (Genesis 1:5). It seems that before Creation there was no time and, of course, no space. Before the first day, it was nothing.

Behind the Hebrew Bible is the everlasting human desire started in times immemorial of attempts to understand where the world came from, where it is going, and why, as well as what is driving the grand machinery of the universe. The relation between reason and existence, spirit and nature, is not neglected at all in the Hebrew Bible. No math or other apparatus is used, and we cannot find mythical figures or stories introduced for any explanation throughout all of Genesis. The Hebrew Bible doesn't deal with the physical world as a hierarchy of structures, as physics does. Everything is done to honor truth and beauty, principles that lead to life and creation, not destruction or confusion. No contradictions between facts and fundamentals can be found.

Sometimes the Hebrew Bible is directly assaulted on the evolution front. Those who do not know the Hebrew text or misinterpret it cannot understand how deep is embedded in the Book of Books such a concept. For instance, it is enough to quote, "Don't be proud of yourself human being, since even the worm was created before you. "In our days everyone knows that ontogeny repeats phylogeny; that means that the development or course of development of an individual organism passes through all phases that the considered individual organism passed in its evolution during the geological eras.

Adopting another point of view, the building pattern of every being, starting with the simplest one, is emphasized in all stages of the most evolved beings, including ourselves. Only via abstractions, deeply ingrained in the Book of Books, could, and can, science be pushed forward as well as the knowledge of unity of space and time, mind and matter, man and nature.

An aspect of modern science is the fact that it has shown that almost all dynamic systems are susceptible to chaos. From a holistic point of view, the universe is a dynamic system where forces of different kinds are at work. From a human point of view, the word chaos implies something destructive, a senseless outcome, but there is a creative aspect connected to it too. We are able to understand much better the statement of the first book of the Hebrew Bible mentioned above: at the beginning it was a chaos. Today we know that the random element endows a chaotic system with a certain freedom to explore a vast range of behavior patterns. The universe as a physical system behaves as though it had its own most powerful computer, making (most of the time) the right choices from the multitude of possibilities. The vast machinery of the universe that has to handle multitudes of random elements seems to us like an "open immense box;" black up to yesterday, able to store, mix, and give new levels of a complex variety, imposing for us to forecast and governed with great skill by the most powerful computer of the universe which, among other tasks, creates, makes up, and exceeds any guess or capability of a finite intelligence.

The physical conditions necessary for the occurrence of life as we know it are extremely stringent. Indeed, the biochemical reactions essential to life depend sensitively on the energies of the molecular states involved; these, in turn, are very sensitive to the exact value of the electron mass and charge as well as other factors. If the electron charge were slightly different from what it is, the biochemistry we know could not exist. The development of life apparently requires not only precise chemical conditions, but also the right distribution of incident radiation.

Here, some other aspects intervene. For instance, if the ratio of electromagnetic and gravitational interaction constants were only slightly different from what it is, our sun would be unable to provide the correct mix. Therefore, in a world with a structure different from ours, no form of life as we know it would be able to exist. A list could be set up and multiplied endlessly, showing how every physical constant has to have the known value, or one very close to it. But the "Great

Manipulator" or "Universal Supercomputer," according to the atheistic point of view, is able to select the essence from the chaotic multitude of facts and produce well-ordered results, guiding us in time from the past toward the future. Indeed, we know evolution produces diversity, and diversity is characterized by lack of standardization, regularity, orderliness, homogeneity, and conformity. But as evolution produces diversity, diversity is the natural order of things.

On the scale of evolution, the Jews were chosen by what the atheist would like to call the "Great Manipulator" of that huge machinery called universe. They were chosen to bear His laws and, as a result, they met all kind of adversities in diverse and uneven situations, practically in every corner of the earth.

Disenfranchised by sanctimonious representatives of different nations who had no compunction about killing human beings and transforming them into industrial products, the Jew survived. To do this, he needed the strength to solve complicated problems in the senseless innumerable accusations over the centuries and millennia of persecution. What makes the Jews a unique and dynamic nation is the powerful, unseen force which was always behind them, which gave them the skill and strength to get and maintain the necessary dynamism. The Jewish tendency and legacy is, and always was, directed toward quality, that distinguished attribute that is highly desirable in any field, including science.

For the Jewish people, the eternal source of inspiration, energy, high principles, and invariant basic elements is in their Torah; it does not matter if some of them do not recognize this. This is why the Jew became a useful person, hated for his ability to survive but serviceable for a beneficial end because of his qualities which made him able to move through history, maintaining his identity unaltered. The Jews succeeded in surviving history itself. The Jews are the only people now living who recall and lament inflictions suffered at the hands of powers whose pride bit the dust thousands of years ago.

For instance, Mark Twain made the following observation: "The Egyptian, the Babylonian, and the Persian rose, filled the planet with sound and splendor, they faded to dreamstuff and passed away; the Greek and Roman followed and made a vast noise, and they are gone; other peoples have sprung up and held their torch high for a time, but it burned out, and they sit in the twilight now or have vanished. The Jew saw them all, beat them all, and is now what he always was, exhibiting no decadence, no infirmities of age, no weakening of his past, no slowing of his energies, no dulling of his alert and aggressive mind. All things are mortal but the Jew: other forces pass, but he remains. What is the secret of his immortality?"[1]

The Jewish I.D. card, as well as their strength, the proof of ownership of their indisputable patch of land on the surface of the earth, is the Hebrew Bible, venerated directly or indirectly by the entire civilized world. The Hebrew Bible shows the unique bond between the Israelite and the Land of Israel. One of the Torah's major motifs repeated in our prayers, benedictions and festivals, is the indestructible relation between the Jewish people and the Land. During every significant prayer, from the daily Amidah to the Grace After Meals, the Jew emphasizes the tie between the land and the people, the people and the land. The Book of Books starts with the beginning of our world (chapter 4) and it indicates how the superiorly organized beings should behave in their environment. Despite its complex structure, the Hebrew Bible

1 See Mark Twain, Harper's magazine, September 1899.

has an undeniable perfection based on its backbone of understanding. It has a rare quality that excites all of one's attention because of its permanence for the man in the street, and its enduring freshness for those who have the background necessary to follow that proof. This is why it excites the interest of professionals of the highest intellectual background (atheists or not) as well as the interest of the simple believer. We may see it as a key to human understanding since it also contains the most ardent questions raised by humans confronted by the mysteries of their existence, worthy of intellectual inquiry and searching for an understanding of nature, man, and society. This is why there was no progressive vanguard without the presence of some of the children of Israel.

The tiny seeds of democracy, freedom, and justice, present though scarce throughout the world, were abundant in Jewish law, mind, and action. These seeds germinated and grew in the robust Jewish soul and mind for millennia, being continually fostered by the invariance of the basic elements of the Hebrew Bible. The courageous Jewish mind did not hesitate to cut against the grain of their oppressors, even when they were enslaved. These men and women succeeded in breathing hope and life into all generations of the human race. We know very well their rewards. It is enough to look back to World War II in order to discover the terrible truth. But this is what we are. A small people forged by the fire of knowledge based on the enlightened eternal law of our great leader Moses and his eternal teachings which, when adopted by us, became a catalyst of the entire world. The entire basis of modern social ethics derives from the Hebrew Bible carried with stubbornness by the members of Jewish communities in each corner of the terra.

The strength of our people was built upon an inner sense of self-worth, of being chosen and unique. It encompassed an iron determination to build, create, prosper, and survive no matter what the odds or hindrances. Our strength was built upon a vision of a better world with a bright future. It provided strength when we were physically weak and persecuted.

Finally, we would like to express the hope that the reader understood the double meaning of one of the Hebrew Bible's names: It is a Book of Books! The first meaning is at everybody's fingertips—a number of books are included within its pages. But last, and not least, the more subtle aspect may appear now: It is a book which by its basic axiomatic structure and content cannot be contradicted even by modern science.[2] Indeed, the Bible starts with the description of Creation, that in fact means with physical science. But one of the great doubts raised by unbelievers was related to the beginning of our world. They maintained that such an event didn't exist. Now, starting with 1965, there is a scientific proof that such a beginning took place in the remote past. As we may recall, (chapter 4 fig. 2), shows how the entire humanity has the same ancestors. Of course the image is very suggestive for everybody's background. But in our days, science shows how the basic elements of life as we know it were cooked up deep inside shining stars emphasizing the unity of our world. In other words, all of us are made up, in a very real sense, from stardust.

What mind could have such a vision able to open vistas over centuries and millennia?

[2] All quotations regarding the Book of Books can be easily found in the King James version.

Appendix A

As we mentioned at the beginning of this book, we do not want to deny, misinform, or ask somebody to believe and not search. This is why we want to give the opportunity to our reader to compare, measure, think, and discover the truth which has been distorted many times. It is one of our aims to give here the Christian version out of the original Decalogue, presented by Moses to his people seven weeks after Passover, during the emotional ceremony that took place more than three thousand years ago at the foot of Mount Sinai, a place that belonged to nobody, as a signal to the entire human body, to underscore the simple fact that their basic content is for any human community that wants to live in peace and respect with its fellows.

Taking into account the well-known fact that the first Christians considered themselves as belonging to the Israelite fold, they used the same axioms, untouched. Only after their definite separation from the Israelites, that took place much later than the official one manifested in front of the Roman authorities,[1] only then were some elements omitted for the Europeans and others completely modified. No wonder nobody dared to touch the Ten Commandments; this wasn't an easy task at all, since no human being could have the authority to change the Mosaic basic guidance. Then Paul of Tarus did it in the name of Joshua of Nazareth God's son. *As the* closest relative of the Almighty, he considered such a change admissable. In the following, we are going to mention all ten axioms in the modified version, and we will indicate where and when

---

[1] The Jews started to be persecuted because of their contined uprising against Rome. Then the Christians began to present themselves as not being Jewish, since they made converts while the Jews did not.

changes occurred:

1. I am the Lord your God, you shall not have other gods beside me. (The second part of the postulate, presented by Moses, has been eliminated.)

2. You shall not make yourself idols in the shape of anything; you shall not bow down nor worship them. (The last part of the postulate, presented by Moses, has been neglected.)

3. You shall not utter the name of the Lord your God in vain. (The last part of the postulate, presented by Moses, has been neglected.)

4. Remember the Sabbath, to keep it holy. Six days you shall labor, but the seventh day is a day of rest and in honor of the lord your God, you shall not do any work. (In the first part Sabbath, which in Hebrew means rest, is replaced by Sunday. In the second part, explicit, important items presented below were omitted.)

[For instance, you shall not do any work, as specified above, neither you, nor your son, nor your daughter, nor your male nor female servant, nor your cattle, nor the stranger who is within your gates; for six days the Lord made the heavens, the earth, the sea, and all they contain, and rested on the seventh day; therefore the Lord blessed the Sabbath day and hallowed it.]

As we can see the original was changed twice.

5. Honor your father and your mother, that you may live long on the surface of the earth.

(The last part of the original version has been modified. Indeed, the original said: "Honor your father and your mother, that you may live long in the land which the Lord your God is giving you.")

6. You shall not murder.

7. You shall not commit adultery.

8. You shall not steal.

9. You shall not testify falsely against your neighbor.
10. You shall not covet your neighbor's house. (The last part of the original version has been neglected.) For comparison please see chapter two.

Appendix B

According to our ancient tradition, the Jews are the offspring of the twelve sons of Jacob, the third Jewish patriarch.The sons formed the twelve Jewish tribes.
The twelve tribes are:

Reuben	Judah	Dan	Asher
Simeon	Issachar	Naphtali	Joseph
Levi	Zebulun	Gad	Benjamin

The tribes Reuben, Gad, and half of the Manassah tribe (one of Joseph's two sons) dwelled on the eastern part of the Jordan River known today as the Jordanian Kingdom. It is that territory of 90,000 square km cut off by Winston Churchill from the mainland of Israel in 1921. On the west bank of the Jordan River, up to less than 30 km from Damascus, each tribe received a patch of land with two exceptions: the Levites and the Cohanim, since together they had to take care of the legislative aspects of Jewish life in the entire country.[1]

The Jews lived from the beginning on that territory, their house, their home, following their religion, and using their Hebrew language in which even God had spoken for the first time to mankind.

---

[1]The children of Israel were divided into three casts: Cohanim, the descendants of Aaron (Moses' brother), the Levites, the helpers of the Cohanim, and the so-called Israelites, that form the majority of the people of Israel. The Cohanim represented the executive power. They had to take care of the way the Mosaic law is applied (since Moses represented the legislative power of the Israelite tribes). As we can see, the Jews organized themselves like in modern time. In each state must exist a legislative power and an executive one.This division has been maintained along history, and each member of a Jewish community knows the cast to which he/she belongs. No privileges were accorded to anyone.

Appendix C

The HEBREW BIBLE

- **The Five Books of Moses** — THE TORAH
  - [GENESIS] → BERESHITH
  - [EXODUS] → SHEMOTH
  - [LEVITICUS] → VAYIKRA
  - [NUMBERS] → BAMIDBAR
  - [DEUTERONOMY] → DEVARIM
- **The PROPHETS**
  - **The EARLIER PROPHETS 6 BOOKS**
    - JOSHUA
    - JUDGES
    - I SAMUEL
    - II SAMUEL
    - I KINGS
    - II KINGS
  - **The LATER PROPHETS 15 BOOKS**
    - ISAIAH
    - JEREMIAH
    - EZEKIEL
    - HOSEA
    - JOEL
    - AMOS
    - OBADIAH
    - JONAH
    - MICAH
    - NAHUM
    - HABAKKUK
    - ZEPHANIAH
    - HAGGAI
    - ZECHARIAH
    - MALACHI
- **WRITINGS 13 BOOKS** — KETUBIM
  - PSALMS
  - PROVERBS
  - JOB
  - SONG OF SONGS
  - RUTH
  - LAMENTATIONS
  - ECCLESIASTES
  - ESTHER
  - DANIEL
  - EZRA
  - NEHEMIAH
  - ICHRONICLES

39 Books

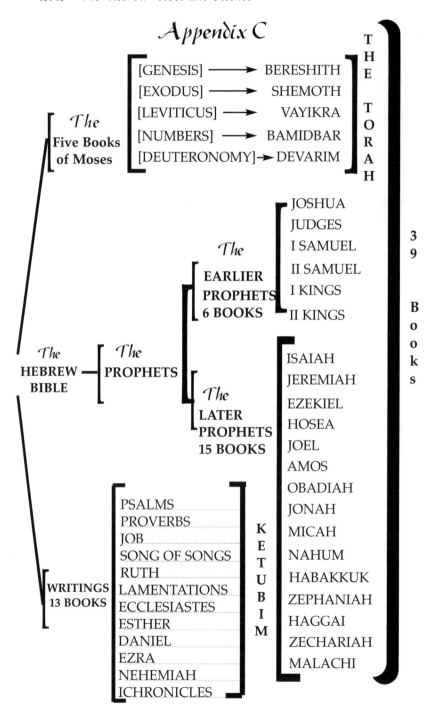

A book is their fatherland, their possession,
their ruler, their fortune and misfortune… From here they cannot be driven out.

— Heinrich Heine

Appendix D

Our Intention is to mention here different Jewish writings based on the Hebrew Bible. We want to present them briefly, since the reader has to be able to grasp the true research made by our people in this field, during its wandering in different countries and continents, and having sometimes to work under the most difficult conditions possible to be imagined by a human being. We consider that those writings are of major importance for the Jewish people first, and by their content, for the entire human race.

Of course, the first one that constitutes the fundamentals of all the others is the Torah, which comprises Moses' five books. Since the Torah is considered the backbone of the Hebrew Bible, we present how many times each letter of the Hebrew alphabet is used in writing the Torah as well as the total number of letters used (see table on the following page).

ד	ג	ב	א
7,032	2,109	16,344	27,057
ח	ז	ו	ה
7,186	2,198	30,513	28,052
ך	כ	י	ט
3,350	8,610	31,530	1,802
נ	ם	מ	ל
9,854	10,623	14,472	21,570
פ	ע	ס	ן
3,976	11,247	1,833	4,257
ק	ץ	צ	ף
4,694	1,067	2,985	834
	ת	ש	ר
	17,949	15,596	18,128

Under each letter of the Hebrew Alphabet is the number of times it appears in the Torah

total 304,868

The Torah became the basic guide for the religious and nonreligious Jew if he tried to read and understand what was written in it. The Hebrew Bible, based on the Torah, constituted the powerful root which gave the impetus and material needed by the Jew to survive in any part of the world. Like any bank of data regarding scientific research, we find here a source of knowledge and inspiration, being a guide in finding the right way in order to satisfy the necessities of the human element that belong to a social organized body. As is well known, social conditions are not ossified once for all. They are changing continuously, and the perpetually moving human mind looks for new insights in order to successfully apply his knowledge to the new given conditions. So a new Hebrew biblical creation was born called Midrash, which means exposition. It is a homiletic commentary on the Hebrew Bible canon, being divided into:

- legal and ritual laws (Halakhah), and
- legendary, moralizing, folkloristic, and anecdotal parts (Haggadah).

New ideas connected with daily necessities are claiming new insights. Then our Eternal Book, the Torah, has been approached with new tools of logic and science. So new wells in the Mosaic text have been discovered. The new fertile method (200 BC) was called Mishnah, which means repetition. The creators of the new branch of the Hebrew Bible study wanted to underline the fact that they do not bring in something extra; it is the same body of knowledge reinterpreted in the given conditions.

In other words, the Torah given to man has the solutions needed, but man has to perceive the truth and that cannot be done at once. The depth exists, but human beings, by research, can penetrate that depth and become beneficiaries. It is a basic compilation of legislation on Torah principles, concluded about 210 BC by Rabbi Judah the prince.

The Jews were spread out in the entire Roman Empire after the third Jewish revolt.(130 A. C.) New problems were raised, and so a new branch of biblical research was created, in order to add more responses. The new branch was called Gemara, or supplement of study. A series of brilliant expounders elevated the Gamara to a high status. The new Gemara was carried to all corners of the Jewish world, practically to every part of our terra. All the aforementioned body of study and achievement we call Talmud; these designed the laws which permitted the Jew to continue to live not only as a Jew but as a universal man. Therefore, the Jews in all lands symbolized mankind split into national entities.

Then laws had to be formulated to enable all national entities to live together in a united enclave of manhood. The ideas launched by the Talmud crystallized the universal concept of government according to Isaiah's dreams of the brotherhood of man. But life doesn't stand still. In the fifteenth and sixteenth centuries, when the Christian horizons expanded from state to continent and eventually to world size, the Jewish world shrank to a continent, to a country, to a province, to a city and, in a painful way, to a ghetto. In the new conditions, the Talmud had to answer questions raised by daily existence.

The task was accomplished by one of Judaism's gentlest scholars, Joseph Caro of Toledo, Spain (1488 – 1575). He was caught by the wave of Spanish expulsion of Jews in 1492. After a short time in Constantinople, he resettled with his parents in the territory called by the Jewish enemies Palestine, where he moved north of Jerusalem to the city known as Safed.

Caro wrote "*Everyman's Talmud,*" published in 1565, and known under the name of *Schulchan Aruch,* which means the prepared table. Using Caro's masterpiece, every Jew could help himself to the appropraite law. Every Jew could find out the mysteries of the Talmud codified, clarified, digested, and indexed. Now any Jew could know like any scholar, what to do in a required condition and so every Jewish community could have self-government.

The usefulness of *"Everyman's Talmud"* played an important role even in the Napoleonic era, when the walls of the ghetto were shattered. The students of the Talmud studied subtle rules of law and logic, and that acquired knowledge gave them the needed background to think in abstract terms in order to find solutions to complicated problems in the new careers that they would embrace. Thus, a large segment of them assimilated from their study the love of justice, which explains why they become idealists who could be found in any corner of our terra where a movement for a better world was undertaken (this is the explanation why during the fight for freedom in different corners of our world, the Jews couldn't miss any barricade). Others became philosophers and writers, and another large segment oriented themselves toward the world of abtractions; thus the subtle world of study and interpretations prepared them for theoretical physics and abstract mathematics, where they brought, and continue to bring in, new and important contributions.

In Germany, before Hitler came to power, the Jews, who represented less than 1 percent of the entire population, succeeded in giving to their adopted country and its honor more than 12 percent of the Nobel Prize winners. For example, the first German poet to win the Nobel Prize for literature, in 1910, was Paul Heyse, a German Jew. In this consisted the damage and danger presented by the Jews to their countrymen, the "pure Aryans" of German descent. This is why they committed the most horrible crimes against them known in history.

Appendix E

We would like to mention some kings of Israel since a large segment of our youth thinks that only Saul, David and Solomon were at the helm of our nation. But other interesting personalities from our past remain in a curiously inexplicable, dark shadow of Jewish history. We intend to dust off those forgotten pages of history and to show them to our reader in full light. Each one of these kings had something to say during critical moments of our agitated history.

Of course, the first Jewish king was Saul (eleventh century B.C.). Aside from the fact that he was the first Jewish king, anointed by the prophet Samuel, he gets little special credit. He died in battle at Gilboa. David, the second king of the united Jewish kingdom (about 1000 B.C.), distinguished himself by the following positive deeds:

- He made Jerusalem the political capital of the Jewish nation,
- He planned the Temple for that city,
- He enshrined the ark of the twelve tribes of Israel, the symbol of national unity, in Jerusalem.

David was a great patriot, talented ruler, never defeated on the battlefield; a profoundly religious man, he tried to inscribe the state of Jewish affairs on the curve of democracy according to the tradition required by Jewish law. His work on internal and external policy was unabated. As with any human being, he was not without passion, and it was that which drove him eventually to commit inadmissible deeds. Although some people criticize him for those deeds, he remains the poet king and harpist, who according to tradition, wrote the psalms. Under his rule were reached and defended all borders of the "Promised Land." But in order to defend his country and its borders, he had to kill many people during his eighteen wars, all victorious for him. As a faithful Jew, he always refused to go beyond those borders. However, when an enemy attacked his country, in order to defend it and to defeat that enemy David's army was forced to exceed the borders on the battlefield; but finally, the adversary had only to pay a tribute for his aggression.

In the historical context in which David became king, he did the best possible job. But his desire was to raise a permanent building for worship of the unique invisible God, the only parameter on which the universe depends on. But according to Jewish tradition the Jewish universal God is against war and destruction; the Temple itself had to be dedicated to peace. As a very religious person he, a warrior, couldn't allow himself to raise such a monument. However, he prepared everything to start and complete the building, the task that was

---

[1]Many years after the death of Muhammad, the founder of Isalm, his followers made up a story, according to which Muhammed, who moved from Mecca to Medina, two well known localities in Saudi Arabia , started his journey to heaven from Jerusalem, from the exact place where the Jewish altar for worshiping the unique God had been located. The journey occurred during one night from Medina to Jerusalem. The Islamic conquerors looked for a religious justification in order to perform one of the greatest profanations in history. They built a mosque exactly on the place where, according to tradition, was the place the altar of King David's temple, raised by his son Solomon. This became suddenly a holy place for them, the first after Medina (approximately 900 years after Muhammad's death). But when the Muslims on the Temple Mount perform their prayers, they face Mecca. On the other hand, the Koran (SURA V, "The Table", as we specified in a footnote of the main text) states clearly that Allah assigned the Holy Land to the Jews but when something has to be grabbed from the Jews, even the Koran is suddenly forgotten.. Of course, the profanation has a certain meaning. Indeed, if you Jews want to worship your god in your ancestral land and place, you must do it via Islam. If you Christians want to be in those places where your leader made up his backround and dwelled, you may do it, but only via Islam, the true believer's creed (since the Christians are called by the Muslims, the unbelievers). No psychological, emotional, judicial, or any possible connection exists between Jerusalem, "Palestine" in general, or any special or particular place in the HolyLand and the Muslim conquerors.

entrusted to his son Solomon, whose reign was based on diplomacy rather than on military confrontations. Solomon never fought any wars; therefore, no people were killed under his command or by any of his generals. Before the Temple was built, the ark was kept in a special tent. Solomon enshrined it in the Temple. Jerusalem became the symbol of Judaism and later of another religion Christianity.

The claim of some religious leaders that the city of Jerusalem is a symbol of Islam, too, is based on acts that constitute a profanation for the Jews and Christian faith.[1]

Solomon was a great ruler and personality of his time, and left his stamp on Israel and the world. He reorganized Israel and reformed its government, sponsored true expeditions of discovery as far as West Africa and India. He encouraged architecture, and his name betokens a lover of peace. He achieved wealth and wisdom. His reputed knowledge of natural history made him to be considered ruler not only of men but of the spirits of the air and waters. Born in Jerusalem, he made it a famed religious and literary center. He has always been the symbol of a wise monarch. His famous wisdom penetrated all levels of social layers, far beyond the Jewish faith. However, he had his weaknesses, too, in the area of human passions. The famous harem of a thousand wives was inadmissible according to the Jewish law. But his behavior has to be judged in the context of that time. On the other hand, he wanted to fulfill his father's desire: to start and finish the house of worship of the unique invisible God. He could acquire the needed peace, by peaceful specific means of his time. Then for his harem he also acquired, among other women, the daughter of the Egyptian king, etc. The Jewish people praised his wisdom and good deeds, but they didn't forget to criticize the negative aspects of his activity, such as the royal harem made up of women of different nationalities, according to his diplomatic maneuvers. Solomon died in 931 B.C.

Rehoboam, Solomon's son, succeeded him to the throne (930–913 B.C.), but he remained the king over Judah, the southern part of the country. The Hebrew Bible (I Kings 12:1–15) tells us about the historic meeting between the free men of Israel, who asserted the democratic principle, that the ruler is the servant of the people he rules, when Rehoboam discarded that principle. He simply refused to listen to the spokesman for the elders, Jeroboam, a representative of the Israelite tribes. In order to enforce his point of view he sent an army against Israel which was decisively defeated. The practical result of such an attitude was that one year after the death of the "King of Wisdom," Solomon, the Jewish kingdom was divided into two states: Judah in the southern part, and Israel in the northern part. Israel comprised roughly ten out of twelve Jewish tribes and Judah the other two. But matters were not settled so simply. Inded, a civil war was started by Rehoboam's opposition to democracy, and the civil strife lasted for one hundred years. After the breakup of the united Jewish state, many other kings ruled Israel and Judah. Jeroboam became the first king of Israel when the schism of the united Jewish kingdom occurred (933 B.C.). Up to 866 B.C. a succession of inept rulers brought the northern kingdom of Israel to the brink of chaos. In 866B.C., Omri succeeded first in stopping the civil strife that had broken out in Israel itself; then he smashed the invading armies of half a dozen hostile nations which tried to take advantage of the internal war. His son, Ahab (873–853), organized a resistance against the increasing power of Assyria. The battle took place at Karkar (854 B.C.), in which twelve buffer states organized by Ahab had Jewish battalions in the vanguard. Over 20,000 fighters died in that battle but, when it was over, the Assyrians had suffered a stunning defeat that set their timetable for conquest back an entire century. But Ahab's wife, Jezebel, the daughter of a bestial priest of Sidon, brought disaster to the country after his death. She was called by the Israelites "the harlot of Sidon." The prophet Elijah was one of her strong opponents. He organized a conspiration and anointed a general, Jehu, to lead the revolt against the harlot of Sidom. He succeeded in liquidating all members of the house of Jezebel, and extirpating the worship of Baal which had been introduced under Jezebel's patronage. Half a century of peace and prosperity followed, and the borders of Israel were again put on their historical lines. The cloud that appeared on the horizon was again from Assyria, a mighty power of that time. However, it took Assyria ten years and three kings to vanquish Israel. Only after ten years did Sargon II succeed in capturing Samaria, the capital of Israel (722 B.C.), and he deported the entire population to make sure that the formidable foe that humiliated Assyria for a decade would not be able to revolt again. It is more than likely that a huge segment of the ten tribes of Israel passed the border of the southern Jewish state of Judah seeking asylum and protection in order to avoid deportation. The history of Judah shows similarities with that of Israel's kingdom. However, the Davidic line ruled the country from the time of split (933 B.C.), until her own defeat in 586 B.C., (347 years) when twenty kings of that dynasty each ruled for an average of seventeen years.

To defeat Israel, a small country, it took a mighty power like Assyria a decade and three kings. Now again a small country approximately half of the Jewish nation succeeded in standing up against a tremendous new power: the Babylonian empire. The great wonder for the entire world wasn't that the Babylonians were finally victorious, but that the Jews fought with such great success that they where almost on the verge of claiming victory again but they were overwhelmed by the endless number of enemy soldiers supplied to the battlefield.